The Horse Owner's Preventive Maintenance Handbook

The Horse Owner's Preventive Maintenance Handbook

ELAINE PASCOE

CHARLES SCRIBNER'S SONS / NEW YORK

Library of Congress Cataloging-in-Publication Data

Pascoe, Elaine.
   The horse owner's preventive maintenance handbook.

   Includes index.
   1. Horses.   2. Horses—Diseases—Prevention.
I. Title.
SF285.3.P38   1986   636.1′08′3   86-10162
ISBN 0-684-18400-1

Published simultaneously in Canada
by Collier Macmillan Canada, Inc.

Composition by Maryland Linotype

Manufactured by Fairfield Graphics

Designed by Marek Antoniak

First Edition

Printed in the United States of America.

For Brack

Contents

CHAPTER I

For Want of a Nail...

If you own a horse, you have an investment. You may have bought him for pleasure or for show, in the hope of financial gain or just because you fell in love with him. Whatever your reasons, you probably spent a fair amount of money and expect to spend a good deal more stabling and caring for him. Apart from your financial outlay, if you're like most horse owners you've made an emotional investment as well. You now have an animal that's unique, with talents, appearance, style, and personality all his own. These traits drew you to your horse in the first place, and now they help make you fond of him. There isn't another horse exactly like yours anywhere.

The horse has a natural life span that ranges up to forty years. Knowing that, you might reasonably expect your horse to be a lifetime investment—something that you'll reap benefits from for years to come. There is no reason why this shouldn't be so. It's not unheard of for horses in their twenties to perform well in all kinds of equine sports.

Unfortunately, however, you hear about these horses because they are exceptional. The sad fact is that the typical horse owner has his animal for only a few short years before disease or physical stress ends the horse's useful life. In fact, insurance companies commonly refuse to issue livestock policies on horses over twelve.

It's not that horses are by nature more subject to fatal accidents and diseases than other living things, although such tragedies take their toll. In most cases, the reason is simple: Owners don't know how to ward off the problems that lead to physical breakdowns. A horse is not a car—there is no warranty, and you can't get spare parts. Nonetheless, a horse is a sort of living machine, subject to mechanical wear and tear.

Stress is the villain that cuts short most horses' useful lives, and it can come from any of a number of sources. Exercise stresses muscles and puts pressure on bones and hoofs—too much pressure, and something will give. Meanwhile, the heart and lungs work overtime to fill the horse's vastly increased needs for energy and oxygen. As the horse's muscles tire, the risk of a false step increases, and with it the dangers of a fall, a cut, a pulled tendon, a broken bone. Other factors add stress to stress: Hot weather, for example, forces the heart and lungs to concentrate on regulating the horse's body temperature, leaving him less able to cope with the stress of exercise. And lying in wait at all times is an army of bacteria, viruses, and other infectious agents. When stress lowers the horse's defenses, they seize the opportunity to attack.

Because the horse is a living creature, he can repair much of the damage he sustains. As long as the problems aren't too severe, wounds heal, torn muscles mend, and antibodies fight off infection. But the horse's problems are often complicated by human beings. Nature designed the equine machine to run freely over the plains, not to carry 150 pounds, jump twenty or thirty fences in a row, or stand motionless in a barn for days. Through neglect or simple ignorance, people create many of the problems they would most like to avoid in their horses.

This needn't be so. As with any machine, proper use and preventive maintenance will prolong your horse's life. An old, oft-quoted saying recounts how "for want of a nail, the shoe was lost; for want of the shoe, the horse was lost; for want of the horse, the rider was lost." Manifestly, caring for your horse requires a great deal more than keeping his shoes nailed on. But the point is well taken: The details of daily care will to a large extent determine whether your horse is still carrying you cross-country or into the show ring five or ten years from now.

You can prevent breakdowns and nip problems in the bud. You can even increase your horse's ability to withstand stress. But to do so you have to be knowledgeable. You have to know how your horse is put together and how his systems work, how various kinds of stress affect him, and how you can minimize those forces and maximize his ability to deal with them. You must be able to recognize problems early and take steps to deal with them before they become unmanageable.

The information you need for this isn't esoteric—it isn't guarded by research veterinarians or close-lipped, weathered horsemen. It isn't difficult to master. The problem is that much of the information has been hard to get—a horse doesn't come with an owner's manual or a service schedule. You could hang around barns for half a lifetime, hoping to pick up tips, and gain just as much misinformation as knowledge.

The purpose of this book, then, is to set out in simple terms and handbook form the information you need as a horse owner. That, coupled with a dose of common sense and a dash of luck, should keep your horse going for years to come.

CHAPTER II

The Horse's Infrastructure

The horse is a creature of bone and muscle, and these are the systems most often damaged by stress. There are dozens of time-honored common names for the lamenesses that can lay horses up, many of them more picturesque than descriptive: bog spavin, osselets, ringbone, sidebone, bucked shins, and splints, to pick out just a few. Anyone reviewing such a list might logically assume that horses are prone to a rash of bizarre and exotic ailments. In fact, in many of these conditions the same simple processes of wear and tear are at work —only the sites and the outward manifestations differ.

This section will take a look at how the bones and muscles that form the horse's infrastructure operate and how they can be damaged by these processes. We'll also see how some simple preventive measures can ward off problems.

1. The Framework: Bone

More than any other component, bone makes your horse what he is. The size and shape of his bones are largely responsible

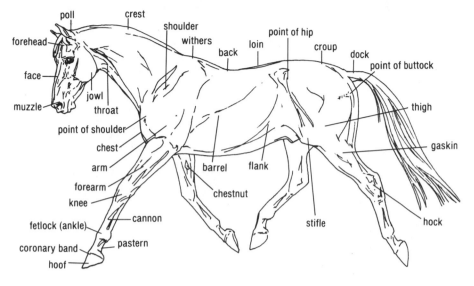

for determining his overall size and his type—elegant thoroughbred, fine-boned Arab, heavy draft, or whatever. The way his skeleton is put together has a lot to do with the way he moves, whether he's a high-stepping saddlebred or a pleasure mount who moves with low, sweeping strides that seem to clip the grass as he goes. Seemingly small differences in the angles of joints mark the difference between a horse with smooth, rocking-chair gaits and one whose choppy way of going makes him a chore to ride.

Bones have a clear-cut mechanical function: They support the horse as the underlying framework of his body, and they give his muscles something to work against. A simple step forward involves dozens of muscles pulling against different rigid bones, lifting them and setting them down, opening and closing the angles between them. Depending on their shape and location, bones may have a second mechanical purpose—protection. The skull, the vertebrae, the ribs, and the major bones of the shoulders and hips guard the horse's vital organs like steel armor, preventing injury.

What makes the collection of armor plates and rigid levers that forms the horse's skeleton so special, however, is that it is alive. Even when it is fully formed, bone is living tissue, capable of growing and changing, becoming stronger or weaker, and repairing itself when it is damaged. It holds vast reservoirs of calcium and other minerals that are needed by the muscles and other body systems. And from their marrow, the horse's bones produce vital components of his blood. Knowing how the living bone functions—and what it is and isn't capable of —can help you prevent many of the tragedies that end horses' useful lives.

HOW BONE DEVELOPS

By the time an equine fetus is a month old, its skeleton has begun to form in accordance with its own genetic blueprint. But bone isn't laid down right away; the skeleton is first roughed out in collagen, the same flexible protein that forms cartilage and gristle. Special body cells migrate to appropriate sites and, taking protein and other building materials from the blood, begin to churn out this substance.

The shape of the collagen map follows the functions that the future bones will serve. Wide membranes of collagen mark the future sites of flat bones such as most of those in the skull, the ones that will have a mostly protective purpose. Strips of cartilage form the advance lines for the long bones such as those of the legs; these bones are columns that will be the main mechanical supports and levers. More cartilage stands in for the short bones—those found in the knee, hock, and other joints—and the specialized irregular bones such as the vertebrae. As each cartilage form becomes larger and thicker, cells toward the inside slow their production. But active construction continues near the surface, where a covering membrane keeps the cells well supplied with blood.

The collagen framework is like an artist's rough sketch. Once it's in place, the long, slow process of converting cartilage to bone begins. The same cells that produced the cartilage now begin to destroy it, leaving an open network in their

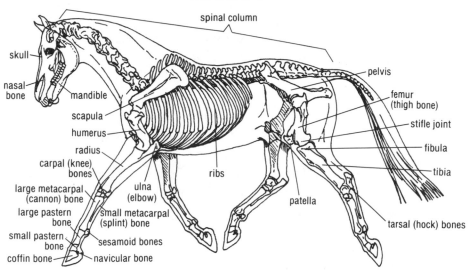

wake. This opens the door for the osteoblasts, bone-forming cells that have proliferated in the membranes outside the cartilage. The osteoblasts invade and revamp the residual cartilage network, creating a tough matrix of protein. Then, again taking materials supplied by blood, they switch roles and begin to encrust the matrix with calcium phosphate and other minerals. Mineral crystals make up about sixty percent of the finished bone's dry weight and are responsible for its rigidity. Without them, your horse's leg would bend like a piece of rubber every time he put weight on it. But the protein matrix is just as essential—it makes the bone resilient. A bone formed only of mineral would snap under a fraction of the horse's weight.

As each osteoblast lays down more minerals, it gradually becomes a prisoner, walled in by its own handiwork. Now called an osteocyte, it remains alive, sending long tendrils through crevices to be nourished by blood vessels. But its work gradually slows as its tiny section of bone is completed. Construction doesn't halt all at once, however; while some cells are finishing their calcification work, others are just beginning to lay down cartilage that will increase the length or diameter of the bone. In some smaller bones the process starts at the middle and works its way out, but in long bones there are typically three growth centers—one at the center, which starts first, and one near each of the extremities, or epiphyses.

At birth the calcification process is nearly complete, but not quite. The foal's bones will continue to grow wider, and they'll grow longer, too, because the epiphyseal growth centers will be active for some time. Most of the growth centers of the small bones (those in the foot and fetlock, for example) are fully calcified, or closed, by the time the horse is a year old. But in the major long bones of the leg—the femur, tibia, and radius—some growth centers can remain open until the horse is two and a half or even three years old. And as long as they are open, they represent weak points in the skeleton.

This is a critical factor for quarter horses and thorough-breds that often begin training, and may even be faced with the stress of a race or some other competition, before the age of three. A training program designed to prevent breakdowns might begin with teaching the horse basic control from the ground, through ground-driving or a similar method, and move on to light mounted work. But to be safe, the trainer might put off difficult work and especially work involving speed or jumping—the two most stressful situations for the skeleton—until the horse is at least two and a half and the owner can be reasonably certain that the bones are fully formed.

THE FINISHED PRODUCT

The average horse has 205 bones in his body, give or take a few vertebrae and a rib or two. Each bone—and each joint—is custom designed for its site and its own specific tasks. While the vertebrae all serve the common purpose of enclosing and protecting the spine, for example, they are not all the same. The atlas vertebra, closest to the head, is shaped to allow the horse to nod his head without moving any other part of his body. The axis vertebra, next in line, has a different shape; it permits him to move his head from side to side.

Similar differences (although not always so pronounced) distinguish the rest of the bones that make up the spinal column. Five more vertebrae complete the neck; their flexible joints allow the horse to arch and stretch it. The eighteen thoracic vertebrae that follow are more tightly bound together and allow very little flexion of the spine. Extensions that poke up like fingers from these vertebrae underlie the withers; below are attached eighteen pairs of ribs. It's the ribs, not the vertebrae, that support the saddle when you ride. Six lumbar vertebrae span the loin, and the next five, the sacral vertebrae, are fused solidly together to form what is in effect a single bone, with its highest point at the croup. The sacral vertebrae are bound tightly to the hip bones, and they are responsible for transmitting the thrust of the horse's powerful hind legs. Last in line are the coccygeal vertebrae, which form the tail. The number varies from fifteen to twenty-one, depending on the breed (thoroughbreds tend to have a few more than Arabs, for example).

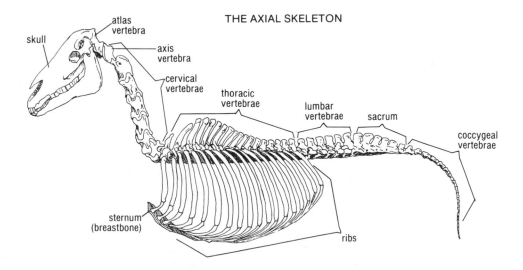

THE AXIAL SKELETON

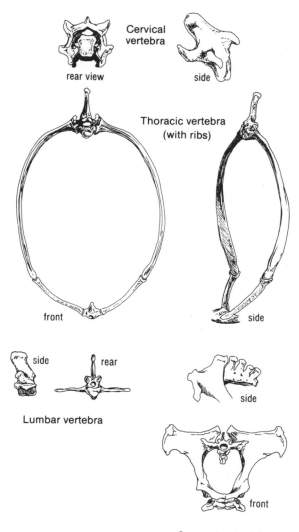

Cervical vertebra

rear view

side

Thoracic vertebra
(with ribs)

front

side

side

rear

Lumbar vertebra

side

Sacrum and pelvis

But of all the bones in the horse's body, the leg bones cause owners the most concern. That's because they are responsible for the horse's movement and, at the same time, are the most prone to injury.

The bones of a horse's limbs are roughly analogous to the bones of your own limbs, but because they have developed for various functions, their shapes and positions are somewhat different. The horse's scapula (similar to your shoulder blade) lies along the side of his chest; it's attached only by muscle (the horse has no collar bone) and moves freely to allow sweeping strides. The humerus (your upper arm) runs back from it at roughly a right angle; it too is bound to the chest by muscle. The leg first breaks free of the chest at the elbow, and it's the radius that forms the upper leg. This is the same bone that, together with the ulna, forms your forearm, but in the horse the ulna is just a short bone fused to the upper end of the radius.

Like your wrist, the knee is a collection of small bones.

BONES OF THE FORELEG

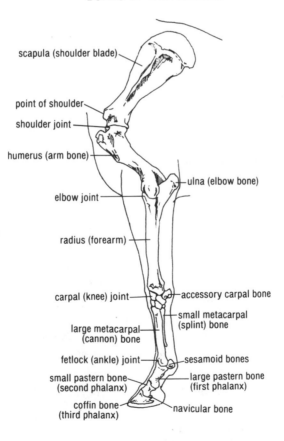

scapula (shoulder blade)

point of shoulder
shoulder joint

humerus (arm bone)

ulna (elbow bone)

elbow joint

radius (forearm)

carpal (knee) joint
accessory carpal bone

small metacarpal
(splint) bone

large metacarpal
(cannon) bone

fetlock (ankle) joint
sesamoid bones

small pastern bone
(second phalanx)
large pastern bone
(first phalanx)

coffin bone
(third phalanx)
navicular bone

Below it are the metacarpals, analogous to the bones in your hand. But the horse has just three of these bones, and only one (the middle one, or cannon bone) does any weight-bearing work; the other two (the splint bones) are slim vestigial remainders of lost toes. At the fetlock, the cannon meets the first phalanx, or long pastern bone; it in turn is followed by the bones that underlie the foot: the second phalanx (short pastern) and the third phalanx (coffin bone). These last three bones together are like the bones in one of your fingers or toes, so in effect the horse is like a ballet dancer, always *en pointe*. Three smaller bones help support the pastern: the sesamoids, a pair of nutlike bones at the back of the fetlock, and the navicular, or distal sesamoid, which lies behind the coffin bone.

The bones of the hind leg take a similar course. The thigh (femur) runs down the side of the body, and the leg breaks free at the stifle, which would be your knee. From there the heavily muscled tibia leads back to the hock, which, like your ankle, is composed of several bones. The metatarsals, phalanges, and sesamoids of the hind leg are similar to those in the fore, except that the hind cannon is longer and rounder than the front.

Just as each bone in the horse's body differs from the next, any given bone is far from uniform and homogenized in composition. A cross section shows that at the center of a long bone, the bone-building osteoblast cells have switched roles again (earning a new name, osteoclasts) and have etched out a hollow cavity to be filled with fatty marrow. As the bone grows wider, this cavity also becomes larger, although not proportionately as much as the overall diameter.

Lining the central cavity of a long bone and filling its ends is a layer of so-called cancellous, or spongy, bone—an airy construction packed with marrow and fat cells. (The centers of short and flat bones are composed entirely of spongy bone.) This porous substance actually makes the bone stronger by

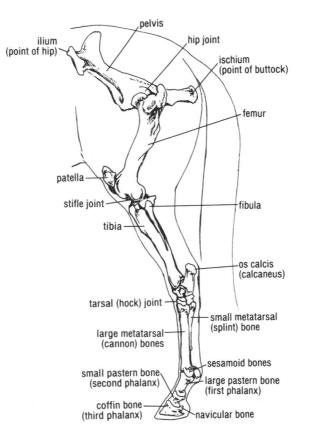

acting as a shock absorber, compressing under weight and springing back into shape when the pressure lets up. The outermost layer of the bone is made up of a dense substance called compact bone; its thickness varies with the amount of stress that the bone will be asked to bear in performing its mechanical functions. Compact bone is remarkably tough. Under direct load-bearing, it can hold up to 20,000 pounds per square inch, and it has a tensile strength of 15,000 pounds per square inch.

The membrane that originally formed around the cartilage remains to wrap the bone, bringing nourishment through its network of blood vessels and nerves. The periosteum, as this membrane is called, also serves as the attachment point for the ligaments, tough collagen fibers that strap bone to bone, and the tendons, which join bone to muscle.

Where bone meets bone at the working joints, the key to smooth operation is lubrication. A slick layer of cartilage coats the ends of bones at joints to provide a friction-free gliding surface. The cartilage at the joint surfaces also acts as a shock absorber; it holds water, which is squeezed out for extra lubrication under pressure. And the entire joint is encased in its own membrane, forming a capsule that is filled with a viscous, lubricating liquid called synovial fluid.

The horse has several ligaments that perform functions other than helping to secure the joints. One of the most important is the suspensory ligament, which runs down the back of the cannon bone and, dividing in two just above the fetlock, wraps around the sesamoids to end at the front of the long pastern bone. It works like a tough rubber sling to support the fetlock under the horse's weight. The plantar ligament, strapped across the back of the hock, performs a similar function for that joint. The check ligaments run from the back of the leg bones to the deep flexor tendon, which also runs down the horse's leg. Besides giving extra support to the tendon,

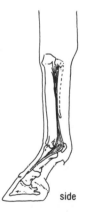 

side   rear

Suspensory ligament

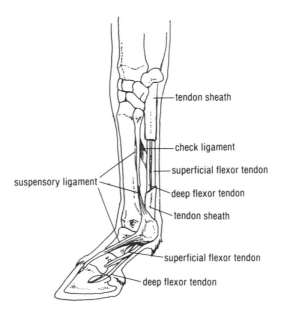

tendon sheath

check ligament

superficial flexor tendon

suspensory ligament

deep flexor tendon

tendon sheath

superficial flexor tendon

deep flexor tendon

these ligaments permit the horse to remain standing when the muscles that control the tendon relax in sleep. The ligamentum nuchae is another with a special job; it fans out from the bony protrusions at the withers to the cervical vertebrae, helping the horse maintain his head carriage.

The specifics of the skeletal system vary from horse to horse, of course, and heredity has a lot to do with that variation. A horse's genes decide whether his back will be short or long, whether his shoulder will be straight or sloping, whether his head will be coarse or attractively shaped, whether his rib cage will spring wide enough to allow full play for his lungs in heavy exercise. Heredity is also an important factor in the size of his bones; compare the cannons of a thoroughbred and a draft horse and you'll see a great difference in width, even if the horses are not all that far apart in height. It may also influence bone density, a quality that isn't so easily judged from outside the horse. A denser bone is less porous, packed with mineral content, and stronger than other bone, but it's no thicker to the eye (or, except in case of extremely porous bone, to the X ray).

But while heredity may determine how a horse's skeleton fits together and may set the parameters for bone size and density, other factors also influence bone. The two most important are nutrition and exercise stress. And unlike heredity, these are not simply cards you're dealt and stuck with. If you understand how they work, you can use them to develop your horse's bone strength to its maximum potential, because even when the last of the ephyseal plates has closed, your horse's bones continue to change and develop.

BONE REMODELING

The bones a horse is born with are only the beginning of the story—they begin to change by the time he is three months old, and they go on changing until sometime between the ages of six and eight. Even after that, subtle alterations allow bone to better perform its two main functions: withstanding stress and serving as a warehouse for the body's supply of calcium and other minerals. The process through which it changes is called bone remodeling.

In a newborn foal, compact bone (the dense outer portion) is formed into a series of layers. As bone remodeling gets under way, the bone cells rework the mineral content of the bone, chewing it away in some areas and re-forming it in others, until they have created a series of tubules called Haversian systems. Each tubule surrounds an open area, called the Haversian canal, through which runs a blood vessel that services that particular area of bone.

The Haversian systems aren't laid down any which way; they follow the lines of whatever stress is placed on the bone. Thus when a horse steps forward and puts his weight on his left fore, for example, the long bones of that leg are subtly twisted and compressed along certain force lines. The bone cells perceive this, although just how they do so is something of a mystery. Some researchers think that a small electrical current gives them the signal, since bone, like quartz and some other materials, produces small amounts of current under pressure. In any case, the bone cells know not only that the bone is under stress but also exactly how it is stressed, and whether or not it is strong enough to withstand that stress. If it is, they do nothing; if it isn't, they begin remodeling.

The process is so closely tuned to stress levels that it can be kicked off by just a minute of unacceptable loading. But the work is slow. The amount of bone formed as a result of one loading incident would be minuscule. But over months of repeated stress along certain lines, the bone changes, first forming its Haversian systems and then becoming increasingly dense in the most highly stressed areas. By the same token, bone that isn't stressed becomes weaker—the body gradually robs it of its mineral content to supply new bone formation and other body functions. If a horse were continually asked to do speed work circling to the left, his bones would gradually change their shape, becoming stronger on the left side (where they had to bear the greatest weight) and weaker on the right. The most rapid and dramatic changes would be seen in a young horse, but even an older one would most likely be affected over time.

Clearly, then, exercise has a lot to do with bone strength. The bones of a jumper's forelegs will become better able to withstand the shock of landing simply by virtue of landing repeatedly. That means that theoretically, at least, you can use exercise to strengthen the skeleton, stressing bones in different ways to kick off the remodeling process. But manipulating bone remodeling to suit your ends is not simple—there is a very small gap between the point where the bone cells consider the stress level to be acceptable and do nothing, and the point where the level is high enough to do serious damage to the bone.

If a bone is massively overloaded, it will shatter. But bones are tough—some laboratory tests have shown that the strongest bones, such as the cannon, can bear as much as fourteen times the horse's weight before they give way. Still, long before this point bone can be damaged, accumulating tiny fissures the way metal does when it is bent repeatedly. Horses that perform in demanding sports such as racing commonly stress their bones to this fatigue zone, and if they are given time to repair the damage, they may actually emerge stronger for it. But if they aren't, the eventual result will be a fracture. Paradoxically, the same mechanical forces also build bone, through its remarkable ability to adapt to stress. The difference is simply one of degree.

BONE PROBLEMS

To get an idea of the kind of stress the bones of a working horse must deal with, consider the cannon bone—not the largest in the horse's body, but one of the most crucial. For the sake of illustration, let's take the left front cannon bone of a racehorse. Forelegs carry more weight than hind (hind legs are the horse's driving engine), so at rest this horse carries, let's say, about 300 pounds on each fore. But the placement of tendons and ligaments and the lever action of the fetlock multiply this force to about 1,500 pounds. That's no problem. When the horse races, however, he leads with his left leg, which now must catch not only his full weight but also all the force of his forward momentum—a combined total in the area of 9,000 or 10,000 pounds.

That's still well within the cannon bone's limit. But problems arise because the horse most likely isn't running dead straight on a perfect, flat surface. He's galloping around curves, on a track that may not be sufficiently banked and may also have soft or hard spots and an uneven surface. So the weight, 9,000 or 10,000 pounds, isn't distributed evenly throughout the bone—it's concentrated in one area. When the horse gallops around a curve to the left, for example, the weight is concentrated on the left side of the bone. Depending on the strength of the individual bone and the number of times it's asked to take this beating, the stress may be too much.

The result may be a fracture—the bone simply cracks under the force of the gallop. The bone may chip, break horizontally or vertically, or, under twisting force, shatter into dozens of fragments that explode out into the surrounding soft tissue. A typical break for this kind of stress would be a slab fracture on the left side of the bone: a vertical slice from the fetlock to a point several inches up the cannon. Or, under somewhat less force, the bone may start to develop microscopic stress cracks. (Just this sort of damage is at work in bucked shins, common to young thoroughbreds in training, in which the cannons become sore.) Unless the cracks are extensive enough to make the horse tender, you may not even be aware that they're developing. But as the stress is repeated, they'll spread, and you may wind up with a full-blown fracture on your hands.

Fortunately, bone has the remarkable ability to heal unblemished: If a fracture heals properly, the bone is quite literally as good as new. But that's a big "if." Bone healing has two essentials, alignment and immobility, and for one reason or another they're often not provided.

Bone mends in much the same way that it forms. In the cannon fracture, for example, the first step is the formation of a cartilage-like lump called a callus, which bridges the gap between the broken ends. The callus is gradually invaded by bone-forming cells that lay down a protein matrix and encrust it with minerals. (Flat bones skip the callus step and form new bone directly.) Then the new bone is remodeled along force lines until it's indistinguishable from the old.

The process takes months, just how many depending on several factors. The bones of young horses heal faster than those of old horses, just as they remodel faster. A big break obviously will take longer to heal than a small chip or crack. If the skin was broken in the accident, infection may enter, creating a whole new set of problems. Infection penetrates the bone through the Haversian canals, and the bone cells respond by walling off these areas and letting them die. The dead tissue can't produce new bone, so it will have to be surgically removed before mending can begin. Another factor is the location of the break—a bone in the upper body heals faster than one in the lower leg or foot because the upper body is better supplied with blood.

Alignment and immobility are the most critical factors, though. If the broken ends aren't lined up and held perfectly still, the bone cells will never be able to form a solid bridge between them. Eventually they'll stop trying, and the healing process will grind to a halt uncompleted. And this is a very real possibility where horses are concerned, because horses by nature won't stand still.

Right after an accident that causes a fracture, pain may be intense enough to keep the horse off the affected limb, and this, coupled with an emergency splint (a bandage reinforced with metal rods or PVC pipe sliced lengthwise in half), can go a long way toward keeping the broken bones from damaging surrounding tissue. But horses aren't very good at hopping around on three legs; even if the horse could stay off the damaged limb for the months of healing, he'd probably develop secondary problems from the strain on his other legs. It's more likely that he'll try to use the broken one, and a cast alone won't be enough to hold the ends in place.

Minor cracks and chips may heal on their own without help, but because of the problems involved in keeping the broken parts in place, many more serious fractures are surgically repaired. The veterinarian screws metal plates or pins directly into the bone, forcing the pieces into alignment and holding them there. Surgery isn't always possible; the bone may be inaccessible, or it may have shattered into too many fragments. The outlook in this case is poor, the reason why many horses who suffer fractures are put down. Depending on the location and severity of the break, though, a cast may hold the bones just enough to allow imperfect healing. The bone may not be strong enough to let the horse perform as an athlete, but he might be sound for breeding or even light pleasure work.

Fractures aren't the only bone problems that develop as a

result of stress. At the joints, cartilage pads are crushed and worn, and ligaments and tendons yank and pull at their points of insertion. As a result, the joint capsules can become inflamed, and as the irritation is repeated again and again, it sets off the bone-healing process—this time in error. This is arthritis, which accounts for many of the lumps and bumps that pop up on a working horse's legs. Bone spavin in the hock, osselets in the fetlock, ringbone in the pastern bones, and splints on the small vestigial bones that parallel the cannon are all examples of new bone laid down in response to irritation. Usually these areas are sore while the new bone is forming, but whether the lumps cause problems after that depends on their specific location. If the lump interferes with the working of a joint or a tendon, the horse may have a continuing lameness. Otherwise, he'll just have a blemish.

Arthritic problems are far more common than fractures, and while they don't have the fracture's ability to instantly cripple a horse, they account for significant numbers of breakdowns. Sometimes an interfering bony lump can be surgically removed, but usually once the joint has seriously deteriorated there's little that can be done. And since arthritis often starts as a mild soreness or stiffness that the horse "works out of" as he warms up, things can get serious before you realize it.

The best course is to take a small lameness seriously, catching the problem early and treating it with rest. Antiinflammatory drugs such as phenylbutazone may help keep joint irritation (and thus, arguably, new bone growth) to a minimum until the flare-up is past, as long as you're careful not to confuse the drug-induced reduction in inflammation with true healing and put the horse back to work too soon. The more powerful steroidal anti-inflammatories are usually avoided because they can actually promote joint degeneration.

A particularly vicious form of arthritis can develop if a joint becomes infected, as it can through a wound. But for the most part the forces that damage bone are mechanical—bone tumors and similar disease conditions are extremely rare.

BUILDING BONE STRENGTH

The exact amount of stress a bone can take depends, of course, on the individual horse. A horse who has gone through a gradual conditioning program in a certain sport—western reining, for example—will have bones well adapted to that work because the remodeling process will have strengthened them. But ask him one day to jump a four-foot fence and you may find that the bones are not strong enough for that work.

Because bone conditioning is site-specific—only the bones that are stressed adapt, and they adapt only in patterns that will let them meet the specific stress—a work program designed to strengthen the horse's skeleton should include maneuvers that the horse will be asked to perform in sport. A cutting horse should be asked to pivot; a jumper, to jump; and the work should be done on the kind of surface the horse will later be asked to perform on. Beyond that, research suggests that the horse will benefit from having his bones stressed in all sorts of ways, with turns, circles, stops, and so on. The stronger the bones are all around, the greater their ability to withstand the sort of sudden, uneven loading that can occur when the horse takes a misstep or lands on uneven ground.

The conditioning work need not—and should not—go on very long, especially early in the program. Once the cells perceive the stress and start remodeling, repeating the strain will only damage the bone, and it will start to get weaker instead of stronger. And various types of work affect the systems in different ways. Researchers have found that bone-building cells kick off the remodeling process when they perceive high strains in a bone, but that the strains can be very brief, perhaps lasting only a minute, to produce the maximum effect. This means that short works at a brisk trot or jumping a few fences will have more effect, where bone is concerned, than hour-long rambles through the countryside. If you give your jumper a half-hour school over fences, probably only the first few minutes will be of any real benefit to his bones.

If the horse isn't exercised, his bones lose strength rapidly. This process is much faster than the strengthening; researchers haven't turned up exact figures yet, but the skeleton may lose mineral content at as high a rate as one percent a week when stress is completely absent. So if your horse has been standing around for a couple of months, you can assume that his bones have lost some of their strength.

Even old horses can correct the situation and lay down new bone, but the process is slow and takes time. Figure on a minimum of three to six months before you start to see any significant effect from your work, and longer if the horse is old, has been out of work a long time, or has never been put in training. Start with short, easy stresses—a few minutes of trot, a crossrail or two—and work up. But remember that repeated poundings won't help.

Another factor that affects bone strength is nutrition. The horse can't build or repair bone unless he has the new materials, including adequate protein, calcium and phosphorus, vitamins A and D, and trace minerals like copper, zinc, and manganese, as well as enough carbohydrates for energy to fuel the process. And since these materials are also used for muscle function and other body processes, the body often gives the bones low priority when it comes to allocating short supplies. In fact, the body will even withdraw from bone minerals that are needed elsewhere. That means that poor nutrition can first affect the skeleton, just the place where you can't see the results.

On the other hand, you can poison your horse by giving him extra doses of vitamins and trace minerals when he doesn't need them. And while a horse is young and growing, you can get into just as much trouble by feeding a diet too rich in energy. This encourages the bones to grow faster and larger, but they gain nothing in strength. Meanwhile, the young horse's rapid increase in body weight can stress the epiphyseal plates, provoking inflammation where bone should be developing. The leg bones can even outstrip the growth of the tendons and ligaments, so that the horse is pulled up on his toes (a condition called contracted tendons).

In nutrition and exercise, then, you have to walk a fine line between too much and too little—and where that line lies depends on what condition your horse's bones are in to begin with. Strength of bone isn't something that can be judged easily from outside the horse, because bone becomes denser, not thicker, as it increases in strength. A number of researchers have made studies using ultrasound scans, in which sound waves sent through bone are used to produce pictures. The scans show considerably more about density than do X rays, but so far these pictures can't be correlated precisely to strength levels.

That doesn't leave horse owners entirely between a rock and a hard place, though. Enough information is available for you to develop exercise and feeding programs that will make maximum use of the remodeling process and pose minimum risk to your horse's bones. Some sample programs are given later in this book.

2. The Power Supply: Muscle

If you've ever watched a newborn foal struggle to his feet, you already know an important fact about the horse's muscles: From birth, he has one of the most highly developed muscle systems of any animal. A foal stands within minutes of birth and is strolling about within a half hour, with four types of muscles working efficiently.

Three of these muscle types work automatically, unseen and unsung. Smooth muscles move food through the foal's digestive system, dilate and contract his blood vessels, and carry out other vital life processes. Cardiac muscle, found only in his heart, will pump away throughout his life. Just under his skin, a thin layer of cutaneous muscles—a type you don't have—is ready to twitch and flick away any unwelcome flies that might alight on his skin.

But it's the skeletal muscles, the fourth type, that take the horse's framework and put it in motion at his will. These are the muscles that concern you most—they make your horse an athlete.

The skeletal muscles are brilliantly designed to perform specific functions in specific ways. Most of these functions—walking, running, grazing—are shared by all horses. But your horse's muscle design also dictates whether he'll be a racer or a weight-puller, a sprinter or a long-distance runner. And the ways in which you ask your horse to use these muscles, along with the care you give them, will help determine how long your horse will continue to do any of these things.

A STUDY IN STREAMLINING

Most of the horse's skeletal muscles are attached to bone so that when they contract, they will flex joints in the most efficient way possible. Two key factors in their efficiency are their shape and location.

MAJOR MUSCLES OF THE HORSE

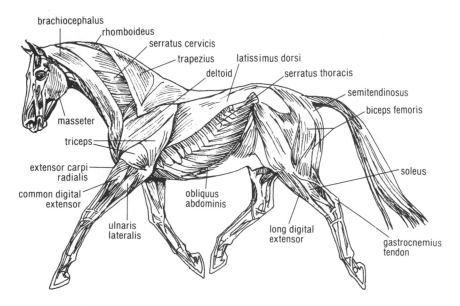

You can see the basic muscle shapes rippling under your horse's coat; which shape a muscle takes depends on the job it has to do. The strongest muscles—for the toughest jobs— are the chunky, triangular muscles that fan out from a single point to a broad attachment. The horse's powerful triceps muscle is an example. Anchored along the shoulder blade, this muscle narrows to exert all its force at the elbow, helping to move the foreleg.

Other muscles, such as the band of abdominal muscles that helps support the horse's internal organs, are wide, flat sheets. Still others are like steel cables—the flexor muscles of the upper leg, for example, and the biceps femoris, a powerful muscle in the hindquarters that takes the shape of three massive ropes.

For the most part, power comes from bulk, not length. Especially at the shoulders and hindquarters, where the major muscles that move the horse forward are found, muscles lie in two and three deep layers. The shoulder muscles in fact form a giant sling for the shoulder blades, which have no

MUSCLE SHAPES

flat
(muscles of the abdomen)

triangular
(triceps)

long
(flexors of the upper leg)

other attachment, supporting them against the horse's weight as he moves forward. Thick ribbons and casings of fascia—which you might know as gristle—reinforce them. These heavy layers of strong tissue have another function, apart from power production and support: They form a cushion three to four inches thick, helping to protect major arteries and nerves underneath.

Despite the bulk, though, the horse is streamlined—the Ferrari of domestic animals. One reason is that some of the muscles work like puppeteers, manipulating bones and joints from above. The muscles that move the lower limbs are located higher up, in the shoulder, forearm, hindquarters, and gaskin. From there they bend knees, hocks, and fetlocks with the help of long ropes—the dense, white, fibrous tendons of the horse's legs. The streamlining is efficient, too: Comparatively short muscle contractions can swing the leg like a pendulum into a long, graceful stride. Where tendons must cross bone surfaces or change direction, they're encased in sheaths that secrete lubricating synovial fluid.

Location is a key to the efficiency of all the horse's muscles: They're located where they can get maximum leverage with minimum effort. And to exert the most powerful tug possible on the levers of the skeleton, most muscles join bones at right angles. To ensure this right-angle junction, many of the horse's joints have bony projections that serve as anchor points for muscles. The most obvious of these bumps is the calcaneus, which protrudes up and back from the hock and anchors the gastrocnemius muscle of the upper hind leg. When the gastrocnemius contracts, it pulls up on this protuberance, and the hock joint straightens out.

The attachments themselves are made by tendons or by aponeuroses, broad sheets of tendonous material. Most muscles produce movement at both points of attachment. For example, the brachiocephalus muscle, which runs from the head down the side of the neck to the shoulder, can turn the head sideways or, by acting on the shoulder rather than the

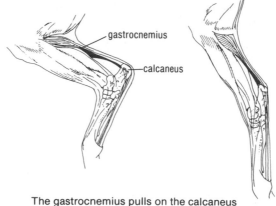

The gastrocnemius pulls on the calcaneus to straighten the hock.

the head, can help move the leg forward. The biceps femoris can raise the hock or lower the croup. The jaw muscles are the most striking exception to this rule of double-ended action; they move only the lower jaw, while the head remains still.

Still, whether they act on one point or more, muscles can do only one thing—pull. They can't push. To get their jobs done, they're set up in opposing teams. In the foreleg, for example, flexor muscles at the back of the leg contract to bend the limb and move it under the horse. Extensor muscles at the front of the leg contract to straighten it and bring it forward. This tug-of-war setup is repeated throughout the horse's body: For nearly every group of muscles, there is an opposing, or antagonist, group.

IN MOTION

The massive muscles of the horse's hindquarters tell you something about his drive train: The horse is a rear-engined animal. His hind legs drive him forward; the forelegs bear the brunt of his weight. To see how the muscle groups carry out these functions, follow the phases of a horse's stride as he gallops across a field.

Each leg moves through three phases: the "swing," or ex-

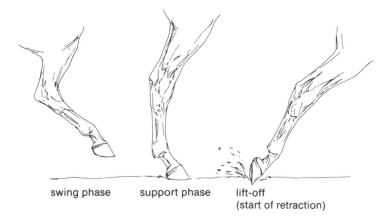

swing phase   support phase   lift-off
(start of retraction)

tension, phase; the support phase; and the retraction phase. At the gallop, there is a moment when all four legs are off the ground in the swing phase at once, their extensor muscles contracting to straighten them and move them forward. If the horse is on the right lead, his left hind will touch the ground and enter the support phase first.

At the moment of impact the muscles in the left leg and hindquarters begin to tense like springs, resisting the horse's weight. As the horse's hips move forward over the left foot, retraction begins. The springs release; the biceps femoris and other muscles of the hindquarters deliver a powerful thrust that drives the horse forward, and the leg lifts off. As it does, the right hind strikes and gathers to deliver a second thrust of its own.

Just as the spring of the right hind is fully loaded, the left fore meets the ground—catching the horse's weight as he is propelled forward. The foreleg's steely extensors, which are laced with tough tendon tissue, help keep it from collapsing under the force, which travels up the leg to be absorbed by the shoulder's muscle sling. By the time the right hind has pushed off, the horse's shoulder has already passed over this leg. Then the shoulder's powerful triceps muscle helps forward momentum by flexing the shoulder and extending the elbow, so that the left fore delivers a thrust of its own as it leaves the ground and enters retraction.

Meanwhile, the right fore has landed and is carrying all of the horse's weight. It's last to lift off, and when it does, the horse is airborne—but only briefly. As soon as each leg has delivered its thrust, flexor muscles spring into action to draw it up under the horse's body. Then the legs move forward and begin to extend to meet the ground again.

It seems easy. A single action, muscle contraction, is responsible for all the horse's power and grace of movement. But the orchestration of that action is far from simple. It's a complex business that takes place deep inside the muscles themselves.

A CLOSER LOOK

The explosive effort that sends your horse spinning into a roll-back or vaulting over a fence begins at a microscopic level. Muscles are made up of fibers, each one a single, slender body cell that in most cases stretches the full length of the muscle. A muscle can contain millions of fibers, held parallel to each other and wrapped into bundles by elastic connective tissue. More connective tissue, or fascia, binds the bundles into mus-

MUSCLE STRUCTURE

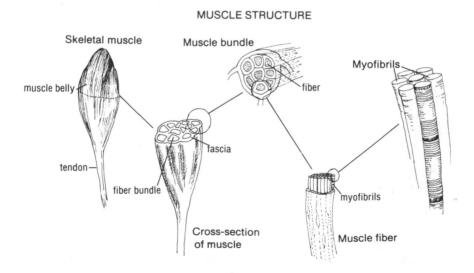

Skeletal muscle Muscle bundle Myofibrils

muscle belly

fiber

tendon

fascia

fiber bundle

Cross-section of muscle

myofibrils

Muscle fiber

cles and lies in sheets between muscles and skin; it's this tissue that turns the individual fibers into a team capable of coordinated effort.

Suspended in the cell plasm of each fiber are nuclei and various agents that help the fiber do its job. The most important of these agents are the contracting mechanisms, the myofibrils. These are strands of protein that run lengthwise through the fiber. Each myofibril contains two proteins, actin and myosin; stacks of actin and myosin filaments alternate down the myofibril's length like stacks of pancakes. Where the two proteins meet, they overlap. The edges of the myosin strands carry microscopic barbs tipped with ATP, a chemical that can release energy almost instantly.

Muscle contraction begins with a simple nerve impulse— the trigger for a complex series of chemical and electrical events within the cell. At the peak of the action, the ATP releases its energy, moving myosin's barbs so that actin fibers are drawn deep into the myosin. To visualize what happens inside the myofibril, think of two combs lying side by side, with the tips of their teeth interlocking. Now push the two combs together, so that one comb's teeth are buried deep within the other's.

MUSCLE CONTRACTION

Contracted

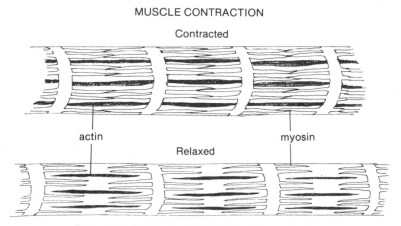

actin

myosin

Relaxed

Filaments of the two proteins actin and myosin draw together to shorten the muscle's length.

As this action is repeated all along the myofibril, the muscle fiber shortens. But only for an instant: In a millisecond, myosin has released its grip on actin and the cell has returned to normal. A sustained contraction requires a volley of nerve signals delivered in rapid succession. And even so, a muscle fiber can maintain contraction only for a matter of seconds before it begins to run out of fuel.

This brief sequence depends completely on a ready supply of a few vital nutrients. Before the muscle can contract, the myosin must be primed with ATP. This is the job of the mitochondria, tiny units in the muscle fiber that make ATP from carbohydrates and fat. Most of their supplies come from a simple sugar, glucose, and free fatty acids. These nutrients reach the cell through a network of capillaries that permeates muscle tissue. But emergency supplies of carbohydrates are also stored within the muscle tissues themselves in the form of glycogen.

In the same way, the electrical and chemical events that spark contraction depend on a few simple elements—sodium, potassium, calcium, and others—called electrolytes. These elements are also delivered by blood, and if they're out of balance, the fiber can't function. The result can be weakness, tremors, or a painful cramp.

PULLING TOGETHER

The action of one fiber, no matter how well fueled and supplied, isn't strong enough to twitch a horse's ear, let alone move him forward. Motion results from the coordinated efforts of millions of fibers. And a team effort on this scale requires organization.

Muscle fibers are organized into teams of ten to a hundred. The team members don't stand side by side; they're scattered throughout the muscle, and there may be hundreds of such teams in a muscle. Each fiber in the unit is connected by a tiny nerve branch to a master neuron—the captain that controls the team.

Motion begins with an order from the horse's brain: Move forward. The command travels down the spinal cord and is relayed on through the appropriate nerve pathways to the master neurons in the muscle. As each master neuron issues its order, all its nerve branches fire at once. The fibers in its unit, wherever they are, contract simultaneously and fully.

Just to walk forward, the horse must coordinate thousands of fibers. Each fiber team must contract at precisely the right time, in precisely the right sequence. But the horse is no more aware of these mechanics than you are: The action is orchestrated from the spinal cord. Nerves in the muscles continually report each leg's position and the state of its muscle fibers, and as these reports reach the spinal cord, the next orders flash back down to the fiber teams.

The brain, as commander-in-chief, is concerned with overall strategy; it can overrule the spinal cord's commands with orders to speed up, slow down, stop, turn, and so on. And by shuffling and redirecting the flow of "contract" orders to the units, the horse can regulate the four key aspects of movement: range, duration, power, and speed.

The range of a horse's stride—or of any movement, for that matter—depends on the number of units that are ordered to fire. If every unit in the horse's extensor muscles contracted with each forward step, his legs would shoot out like a chorus-line dancer's. Instead, the horse fires just enough units to produce the degree of movement required.

Sometimes the result is no movement at all. If just a few units contract, their wholehearted efforts are smothered by the weight of the surrounding, inactive fibers. The contracting fibers struggle against the muscle mass in an isometric exercise, and the muscle as a whole tenses but shortens only slightly. At other times, the contraction of every fiber in the muscle may not be enough to produce the range of movement the horse requires. Then teams in neighboring muscles are ordered to fire. When the horse extends his leg fully forward, for example, the order to contract passes down a sequence of extensor muscles that go off like a chain of firecrackers.

The horse can limit the range of his movements in another way: by ordering opposing muscle groups to fire. If you watch a tense horse trot, you'll see that he shortens his stride—not because he's decided to put out less effort, but because his flexor muscles are stiff and tight and are limiting the action of the extensor muscles. In the same way, a horse advancing gingerly over unsure footing keeps his flexor muscles tense as he moves his leg forward—primed for a quick withdrawal.

The duration of nearly any movement the horse can make is far longer than the split second that it takes for each fiber to contract; even the sustained contraction of a fiber team is little more than a momentary twitching. The horse can maintain movement because most of the time all the units in a muscle don't fire at once. While some twitch, others rest; then the first group rests, and another group twitches.

If you ask your horse for prolonged movement—to hold his hind foot up while you clean it, for example—he's forced to call again and again on the same groups of muscle fibers. Gradually, the fibers use up their energy supplies, and they're

A horse may use flexor and extensor muscles together to limit movement...

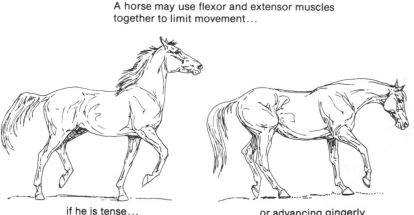

if he is tense...

or advancing gingerly over unsure footing.

not being resupplied quite fast enough to keep up with the horse's repeated commands to twitch. The muscles begin to tire, and the horse tries to drop his leg or lean on you for support.

Power and speed are closely related; both depend on timing. When many master neurons fire simultaneously, millions of fibers contract. The result is an immense effort—the kind of effort you see a draft horse put out against a heavy load. The horse can't keep up this effort very long, though—high power breeds short duration. When a muscle contracts fully, most of its fibers are used. There aren't enough standby fibers to take over the work when the first group tires, and the first group will need time for refueling before it contracts again. At a slow trot, on the other hand, fewer fibers are at work at any one time. There are plenty of standbys available, and the off-duty fibers have time to rest. The horse can keep up this kind of effort almost indefinitely.

To switch from a slow trot to a fast trot, the horse speeds up the sequence of master neuron firing. The faster the firing, the faster the contractions follow one another. But there's a point of no return in speed—at high speeds, the contractions are virtually simultaneous and the muscles begin to tire. Like power, speed can be kept up for only short periods of time. (In fact, high-speed work is very like power work; if you cut the traces of a draft horse just as he strained against his load, the force of his effort would send him shooting forward.)

The ability to fire master neurons in quick sequence won't make a horse a Secretariat, though. The two chief factors that separate the greats of running from the also-rans are the ability to push off hard from the ground and, more important, the ability to recover quickly and make that effort again and again, all the way around the track.

A racehorse with a smooth, straight, efficient stride has a natural advantage because he'll be able to move fast with less effort and thus recover more quickly than another horse. You may not own a racehorse—your horse may never even smell a track. But the same ability to recover is required for almost anything you might ask him to do—cut cattle, jump a course of three-foot fences, carry you on a day-long trail ride. And how well his muscles recover from each effort, great or small, depends largely on how efficiently they use their energy supplies.

NATURAL TALENT

The quarter horse gained fame for bursts of speed at the quarter mile, but at longer distances the thoroughbred outstrips him every time. The Arab is known for endurance; the Clydesdale, for strength and power. What makes these breeds so talented at different types of work?

The answer lies in their muscle fibers. All muscle fibers burn fuel to produce energy, but they don't all do it in the same way. Depending on their type, fibers can produce energy aerobically, burning carbohydrates and fats with oxygen, or anaerobically, without oxygen.

Aerobic energy production is a dream of efficiency. It uses about one-ninth of the fuel the anaerobic method uses to produce a given amount of energy, and fibers recover fully from aerobic contraction in a millisecond. Theoretically, if the horse could supply his muscles with all the oxygen they could ever use for aerobic work, he could gallop until he had used up every available molecule of fuel. The catch is that the oxygen supply is limited. A horse can't work aerobically any faster than his heart and lungs can supply oxygen through the blood. When the average horse reaches a speed of about 200 meters a minute, the muscles start to run out of oxygen faster than the circulatory system can deliver it.

When this happens, the horse switches over to anaerobic energy production. In this method, he uses muscle enzymes to burn his stored reserves of glycogen. He can put out top effort with this method regardless of the oxygen supply, but there are drawbacks. Anaerobic energy production can be kept up only for about three minutes. It's less efficient than the aerobic method because the glycogen isn't burned completely, and it produces toxic waste products—lactic acid and other chemicals—that start to build up in the muscle tissues.

These chemicals interfere with the electrolytes that are essential to muscle contraction, so the muscles start to weaken or cramp. The waste chemicals also make the horse's blood acidic and can damage the fibers themselves. As a result, the horse quickly feels pain and fatigue. He must rest until his circulatory system can catch up, clear out the waste products, and bring fresh supplies of oxygen to the muscle cells.

When the horse switches from the aerobic to the anaerobic method, he calls on different muscle fibers. He has three kinds to choose from: slow-twitch, fast-twitch high-oxidative, and fast-twitch low-oxidative.

Slow-twitch fibers are adept at aerobic energy production, and they're used heavily for long-term, low-power needs— standing up, for example. These fibers are laced with a dense network of blood vessels that deliver ready supplies of glucose and free fatty acids, as well as oxygen. They fire more slowly and can maintain contraction for longer periods of time than the other kinds. Most flat muscles are made up largely of these fibers.

Bunchy muscles contain higher proportions of the two kinds of fast-twitch fibers, both of which contract more quickly than the slow-twitch fibers and can put out more power—for shorter periods of time. Low-oxidative fast-twitch fibers are the anaerobic specialists, packed with stores of glycogen. Their high-oxidative cousins can work with oxygen or without it, depending on the situation, because they have both glycogen stores and ample blood supply lines. These all-around fibers can develop their potential for aerobic or anaerobic work through appropriate training.

All horses have all three types of fibers, and it's thought

that as the level of work increases the horse switches from one type to the next in sequence—from efficient slow-twitch to more powerful fast-twitch high-oxidative to the backstop of fast-twitch low-oxidative. What makes one horse more adept at distance work while another excels at bursts of strength is the proportion of each fiber type in the muscles.

To a degree, you can see the differences in the breeds. An Arab, for example, has long flat muscles that speak for a high percentage of slow-twitch fibers, and thus this breed can put out moderate effort for long periods of time. The bulky muscles of a draft horse or a quarter horse indicate more fast-twitch fibers, and thus a greater ability for short-term, explosive effort. Muscle biopsies show that some quarter horses' muscles are nearly 100 percent fast-twitch fibers, compared to about 85 percent for a typical Arab.

The thoroughbred's muscles fall somewhere between the two—not surprising, when you remember that the thorough-bred was developed by crossing Arabs with heavier breeds—and this helps explain the breed's versatility. Researchers think thoroughbreds have a high proportion of fast-twitch high-oxidative fibers, which can be developed with training to favor distance or high-power work.

You could make a rough judgment of any horse's talent for different kinds of work just by looking at his muscles to see if they are mostly bulky or mostly flat, or, if you wanted to go that far, by having a muscle biopsy done. But in practice, of course, other factors enter in. For one thing, like bones, muscles develop only if they're used.

DAMAGE TO MUSCLE

As with bone, use strengthens muscle—up to a point. Beyond that point, the result is strain. Muscles and tendons can be strained if they are stretched too far, if they are asked to bear too great a load, or if they contract too violently against a fixed object—if the horse kicks a stone wall, for example.

The severity of any strain depends partly on the number of fibers that are damaged and partly on the type of damage that's done. In a simple strain, some muscle fibers are overstretched but the surrounding tissues aren't damaged. There is no internal bleeding. A more violent strain can damage both muscles and tendons. Muscle fibers may be torn in two. Tendons may be irritated, or they may rupture or be pulled from the bone. There may be internal bleeding as well.

In any case, the damaged fibers release chemicals that produce pain and increase the flow of blood and body fluids to the area. Thus the signs of a sprain are the cardinal signs of inflammation: heat, pain, and swelling. If the muscle fibers have been badly torn or if tendons have become detached, the horse won't be able to use the muscle until the strain has healed. If the fiber and tendon damage isn't so extensive, he can use it, but he probably shouldn't. Using the muscle will only compound the damage.

Rest is the best treatment for a strain. Painkillers and nonsteroidal anti-inflammatory drugs will make the horse more comfortable, but as in arthritic conditions they should be used with caution because they mask symptoms. Your only yardstick to the horse's recovery is the sensitivity of the injured area; if the horse is on painkillers, you could easily put him back to work too soon and reinjure the muscle.

Healing time depends on the severity of the injury. Muscle fibers heal in anywhere from a few days to a month; tendons can take much longer. A serious injury such as a bowed tendon—in which the major flexor tendon of the leg is torn, and the resulting swelling produces a characteristic bow behind the cannon—requires a vet's attention and may take up to a year to heal.

Not all tendon injuries are this drastic by any means. For example, windpuffs and thoroughpins are relatively harmless soft swellings at the ankles and hocks. They're caused by fluid that builds up in the synovial sheaths, the smooth casings that enclose the tendons. The initial puffiness may be caused by a

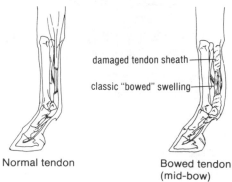

damaged tendon sheath

classic "bowed" swelling

Normal tendon

Bowed tendon
(mid-bow)

mild strain; after that, the sheath is stretched, and it fills up every time the horse works. Unless the area is warm and tender, there's probably no cause for concern.

It is possible for muscle to be microscopically damaged without your being aware of it, though. When the horse works anaerobically, wastes begin to build up in the fibers. They interfere with the chemistry of muscle contraction, and researchers believe that they can actually damage the fibers. In itself, such damage will be quickly repaired once work stops— the circulation catches up, cleans out the waste, and restores needed oxygen, and the job of healing damaged fibers gets under way.

But waste-product buildup has two alternative outcomes, neither of them as cheery. In one, the wastes interfere with contraction to the point that the fibers become inefficient— they're tired. Because his muscles aren't doing their jobs of placing the legs properly and supporting the bone structure, the horse takes a bad step and winds up with a serious injury, a torn tendon or even a fracture.

The other possibility is muscle hyperexcitability, which is more a biochemical than a mechanical outcome of stress. It's linked to chemical imbalances—a depletion of electrolytes, and a high level of waste enzymes—and it can take three forms: thumps, or synchronous diaphragmatic flutter; tying up; and azoturia. Thumps is marked by convulsive twitching of the flanks and abdomen, in time with the heartbeat. Tying up and azoturia are related to each other; the first is stiffness that strikes the horse's hindquarters during a workout, the second a more severe spasm that brings the horse to a standstill and can leave his muscles seriously injured, even scarred.

The switch that kicks on these problems is thought to be an insufficient supply of calcium and potassium, quantities of which can be lost when the horse sweats. When potassium is in short supply, muscles are too excitable—they contract at the drop of a straw. Since this element also helps dilate the blood vessels that lead to the working muscles, oxygen deliveries are reduced. Calcium plays a vital role in relaxing muscle fibers. So when a muscle is deficient in these elements, it contracts too readily, can't get enough oxygen, and can't relax. The spasms themselves close off capillaries in the muscle tissues, choking off blood delivery even more.

Hyperexcitable muscles are usually seen in horses competing in tough sports such as endurance rides and three-day events, where fluid loss is a problem. Riders in these competitions often offer their horses electrolyte solutions at rest stops to restore calcium and potassium (see pages 136–137). But these problems can also strike out-of-shape horses who are allowed to stand in their stalls for a few days and are then put back to work with a bang—in fact, tying up has long been called Monday morning sickness for just this reason. The key here may be diet. Most grains are comparatively low in potassium, compared to hay, so a horse whose diet is largely grain may be deficient in that element.

Whatever the cause, wastes and acids build rapidly in cramped muscles, and damage follows quickly. Hyperexcitability problems demand fast treatment—you should stop work and call the vet immediately. Keep the horse warm—blanket him if necessary—and keep him moving until the vet arrives to keep as much blood as possible flowing to the area. Anti-inflammatory drugs, vitamins, and minerals are often part of the immediate therapy for tying up, but the horse's diet should be scrutinized closely to prevent further attacks. Sometimes horses who tie up persistently improve when a bit of baking soda is added to their feed; the soda seems to reduce the acidity that develops when the horse exercises.

BUILDING MUSCLE

Whether he's a bulldog quarter horse or a sleek thoroughbred, your horse won't realize his muscular potential unless he works at it. Exercise is stress, and up to a point the horse's muscles respond to stress by toughening up.

Exercise has three basic effects. First, as the fibers are used the horse begins to pack more protein into them, and they become thicker and more powerful. Very young horses may even increase the number of their fibers with exercise. (The protein buildup is one reason why the diets of horses in training should include adequate protein, as well as extra carbohydrates for energy and electrolytes for fiber function.) There's an opposite side to that coin, too—when a muscle isn't used, the protein is drawn out and the muscle shrinks. A muscle fiber that isn't used at all—because of nerve damage, for example—will lose its entire contents and atrophy. Once this has happened, the muscle can't be brought back.

Second, exercise improves the delivery of oxygen to the muscles. The heart, which is a muscle itself, is forced to work harder and thus becomes stronger. Meanwhile, exercise expands and enlarges the network of capillaries that feed the muscles; more blood can be pumped with each heartbeat, and the blood reaches the muscles more efficiently. The muscles get more oxygen, so the horse can do more work aerobically before switching to the anaerobic backup. He tires less quickly, and when he does work anaerobically he can recover from it faster.

Third, exercise increases fiber efficiency. Use encourages the horse's system to deposit more energy reserves in the fibers that work hardest. And these fibers become more and more efficient at converting nutrients to energy.

The kind of exercise a horse does determines which fibers will be built up. Long, slow rides—a lot of walking and trotting—encourage the horse to use his slow-twitch muscle fibers. These are the fibers that burn fuel aerobically, with oxygen. The more they're used, the thicker and stronger they become and the more readily they fire. And as the horse calls repeatedly on his fat-storage deposits for the free fatty acids and triglycerides that these fibers burn, these fuels are released more and more readily into the bloodstream. Because his aerobic muscle performance improves, the horse's endurance increases. This kind of work also helps the heart and circulation reach their potential.

Bursts of speed work, on the other hand, call on a different set of fibers—the fast-twitch ones that burn fuel without oxygen—and strengthen them in the same way. The fibers get stronger, and the body is encouraged to provide more fuel (glycogen in this case) for them. But here the potential for damage is greater, because as the horse's anaerobic performance continues, wastes begin to build in the muscles, and fuel supplies run out faster than they can be replaced. This is why speed work is best done in short intervals, with rests in between. Rests allow the horse to clear out the wastes and give the fibers a chance to recuperate before they're stressed again. After a few months of such workouts, you'll see thick, chunky muscles standing out beneath his coat.

Most good training programs include a mixture of both kinds of work, so that the horse will get maximum use from all types of muscle and so that his oxygen delivery system will develop in pace with his muscles. If you keep your horse for general riding, this is all you need to do. But if you have a special activity in mind—jumping or endurance riding, for instance—you can build on this base with workouts that call on the muscles your horse will need in his career. Some halter-horse trainers even back their horses for a part of each training session so they'll develop the full, well-rounded hindquarters that win points in the show ring.

There are no shortcuts in muscle building. Giving the horse anabolic steroids will produce the appearance of strength—thick, bulky muscles that look as though they could carry the horse through anything. These drugs, which are basically male sex hormones, are commonly used by human bodybuilders, as well as some horse trainers. But more muscle mass doesn't necessarily mean better performance; in fact, some researchers think the increased mass is due mostly to water retention in the fibers. And since the bigger muscle mass isn't accompanied by an increase in bone strength or circulation, the horse is ill-equipped to make use of his new physique. In any case, the anabolic steroids often make a horse aggressive and difficult to handle.

How long muscles take to reach peak efficiency through old-fashioned hard work depends on a lot of factors—the kind of work being done, the horse's condition when he starts training, the diet he's getting. Some studies have shown that the fibers themselves can reach their top potential in about a month. But that doesn't mean that you can bring a horse to competitive condition that fast. A full conditioning program has to consider all the other body systems—heart, lungs, bone—as well as muscle tissue. You'll find the outline of such a program later in this book.

CHAPTER III

The Well-Built Horse

Conformation—the way a horse is built—is a key factor in both soundness and athletic ability. Good conformation doesn't guarantee that a horse will be a star performer or sound for life, but it helps. This is why horsemen have long had ideal standards of conformation and continue to search for horses that match them. But the fact of the matter is that no horse is perfect; if such a beast existed, it would literally be beyond price. Moreover, relatively few horses approach the ideal.

Defects in conformation help dictate the sites where breakdowns from exercise stress will be most common. Since the horse carries about sixty percent of his weight on the front limbs, more lameness problems start there than in the hind limbs. The danger areas are the key joints and tendons, whose job it is to deflect the concussion of every stride. And not surprisingly, the danger of breakdown is greater closer to the source of concussion, the ground. When a veterinarian examines a lame horse, he starts at the most likely spot—the foot—and works up.

Yet, barring extreme examples, being cursed with a few

conformational flaws doesn't necessarily doom a horse to a life of lameness or ineptitude. As the saying goes, it's not what you have but what you do with it that counts.

If you're buying a horse, a sound knowledge of conformation will help guide your choice. But that doesn't mean that once the money changes hands and the horse is in your barn you can forget about whatever flaws he has. Perhaps the greatest favor you can do your horse is to respect his individuality—not just his personality, but the physical quirks and oddities that make him different from every other horse. If you're aware of conformational flaws that make certain types of work more difficult for him than for other horses, you can adjust his work accordingly. You may be able to take some preventive steps to give him extra protection against the kinds of stresses he's most susceptible to. And if you're alert to the problems that his conformation makes him prone to, you may be able to detect them early, before they develop into serious, permanent unsoundness.

A WELL-BUILT HORSE

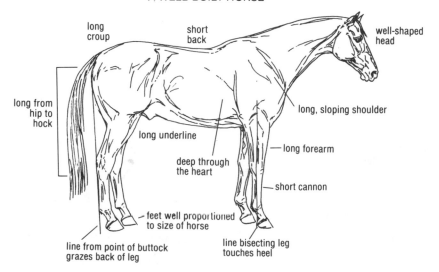

long croup

short back

well-shaped head

long from hip to hock

long underline

long, sloping shoulder

long forearm

deep through the heart

short cannon

feet well proportioned to size of horse

line from point of buttock grazes back of leg

line bisecting leg touches heel

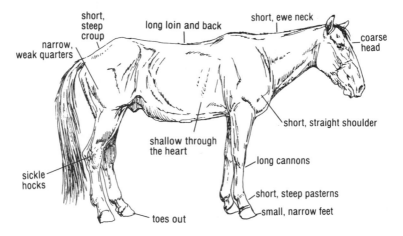

narrow, weak quarters

short, steep croup

long loin and back

short, ewe neck

coarse head

sickle hocks

shallow through the heart

long cannons

short, straight shoulder

short, steep pasterns

small, narrow feet

toes out

1. The Body Beautiful

There is no single conformational standard; differences in the breeds preclude that. Arabians tend to have shorter backs than some other breeds; the quarter horse, a heavier body than the Arabian. But there are general guidelines that apply to all horses. These guidelines concentrate on three areas: proportion, angle, and balance. To see how your horse measures up, you'll have to view him from the front, side, and back; up close and from a distance; and when he's in motion as well as standing still.

HEAD AND NECK

In purely mechanical terms, the horse's head and neck exist to keep him in balance. His natural center of gravity lies behind the withers, somewhat forward of the midpoint of the back. Raising his head helps him shift his weight back; lowering it moves weight forward. If you watch a horse galloping loose in a field, without the interfering weight of a rider, you'll see that he uses his head and neck to counter shifts in weight in the rest of his body.

It stands to reason, then, that the head and neck should be in proportion to the body. A small-bodied horse with a long neck and heavy head will tend to carry more weight than average on his front legs, and they may take more of a pounding as a result. You can help him when you ride by teaching him to travel in a somewhat more collected frame, encouraging him to bring his hind legs up under his body so that they bear their fair share of his weight. The big-bodied, short-necked horse, on the other hand, has another problem: He may not be as agile as a longer-necked horse. He'll be at a disadvantage in events that require quick shifts in balance—jumping a trappy course, for example, or cutting and reining competitions.

The short-necked horse may have a second problem: The neck muscles help move the shoulder forward, so the horse with a shorter than average neck will tend to be short-strided. If he has to take ten strides to cover the same distance that another horse covers in seven or eight, he'll tire faster. But how seriously his short neck limits his endurance depends on a lot of other factors, including his general condition and the rest of his conformation.

Conformation is important in the head itself, and not just because a pretty face is appealing. In fact, a pretty, delicate head often has some serious flaws, especially if it's narrow. Eyes that are set wide apart give the horse the largest field of vision; a horse whose eyes are set close together may shy more because, with his limited field of vision, he can't identify the sources of noises behind him.

A narrow head will also be likely to have narrow nostrils and nasal passages. They'll limit the amount of air the horse draws with each breath and, with that, his stamina in aerobic work. For the horse to get enough air, the throat has to be wide enough to accommodate the windpipe and the esophagus. One old rule of thumb is that a man's closed fist should fit comfortably between the lower jaw bones, at the ends nearest the neck. The horse with the narrow head isn't useless, of course, but you should be aware that he may be at a disadvantage in sports such as endurance and cross-country riding, which require a lot of stamina.

Farther forward in the jaw, it's important that the upper and lower teeth line up. If the horse has an overbite or an underbite, he won't grind his food properly, and much of it may pass through undigested as a result. He may be a poor keeper—requiring more food to keep weight on—and he'll prefer his oats crimped or crushed.

The way the head and neck are joined is important, too. A neck that tapers gradually to meet the head will be able to flex easily at the poll and will allow the horse to move his head freely in all directions. To get an idea of how much freedom of movement your horse has at the poll, place your fingers between the atlas vertebra (which you'll see protruding near the poll) and the back of the lower jaw. Ideally, you should be able to fit two fingers near the top and three farther down. When this space is narrower, the horse's ability to flex at the poll is limited. Chances are that he has a thick throatlatch, too. This conformation may make it hard for him to travel on the bit, or in a collected frame, because when he tries to flex at the neck his breathing is restricted. The same is true for the horse with a ewe neck, which lacks a natural arch (ewe necks

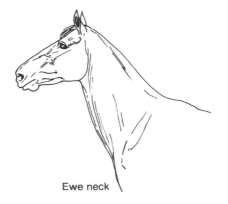

Ewe neck

are usually undermuscled, too, which again limits the horse's stride). A horse with one or the other of these neck faults will be most comfortable if you allow him to carry his head as close to its natural angle as possible.

WITHERS AND SHOULDERS

The way the withers and shoulders are formed sets the stage for the action of the front legs. The shoulder blade is lashed to the withers with muscles and attached more loosely to the thorax farther down, so it can glide freely back and forth as the horse moves. When the withers are prominent and set well back, the shoulder will usually run forward from them at an angle of sixty degrees or less and have a full range of movement. The horse moves forward with long, sweeping strides that cover ground easily. If the withers are flat, on the other hand, the shoulders will often be closer to vertical. Its action will be restricted—a straight-shouldered horse tends to move with short, choppy strides, which are uncomfortable for the rider and tiring for the horse.

A straight shoulder will also absorb shock less well than a sloping one, so the bones and joints of the leg will be more stressed. If your horse has this conformation, you may be able to help by teaching him to bring his hindquarters up under his body as he goes—lightening the front end as he travels will help him lengthen his stride and will take off some of the stress. But you should be aware that he'll probably never develop a flowing stride, and he may always be a bit limited as an athlete. And you need to be on the lookout for the joint and bone problems that stem from too much concussion.

Low withers create another problem: It's hard to keep the saddle in place on the back. The saddle should be positioned just over the back of the withers, where the back is best able to bear weight. You may need a breastplate or even a crupper to keep it from sliding around. On the other hand, high withers can also cause problems. If they're not well padded with muscle on either side, to keep the front of the saddle up and off them, the pommel will continually rub against them and the horse will have saddle sores. A saddle that is cut back over the withers sometimes solves the problem. But high, narrow "knifeblade" withers often come along with other conformation defects, such as a narrow chest.

BACK AND BARREL

Viewed from the side, a well-built horse is close-coupled—that is, the distance from the withers to the croup is short in comparison to the distance from the elbow to the stifle. This conformation goes hand in hand with sloping shoulders, strong hindquarters, and a deep chest. But length of back is relative to the overall size of the horse and the length of his legs. One old yardstick has it that the horse should be square: The distance from the point of the shoulder to the point of the buttocks should roughly equal the height from the withers to the ground.

When a horse has a back that's long in proportion to his body, he may have difficulty with collected work. Long backs often are weak backs, prone to muscle soreness. Be sure that conditioning keeps the muscles over the loin as strong as possible, but proceed slowly and carefully to make sure that you don't strain them with overwork. Long-backed horses also often develop a swing in their strides that leads to interference —their feet brush the opposing legs as they move. A horse whose back is too short, by contrast, is set up for forging, in which the hind feet overtake and strike the front feet in the stride. Bell boots or overreach boots may help; sometimes rolling the toes of the front shoes allows the front feet to break over faster and get out of the way.

The ideal topline is slightly concave behind the withers and slightly convex over the loins. A horse with a flat or roached topline may have less flexibility in his back and therefore lack some agility; a sway back is usually weak and poorly muscled through the loins. In young horses the croup is often higher than the withers, which catch up in height around the age of three or four. Some horsemen like to see hindquarters slightly higher than the forehand in adult horses, too, believing that this gives the horse more driving power. But in general, when the withers and croup are the same height, the horse is in better balance; he isn't forced to carry too much weight on his forehand. A high-crouped horse can be helped back into balance with collected work.

The horse's driving power results more from the way his hindquarters are put together than from their height. The longer and better muscled the quarters, the more power he'll have. The angle from croup to tail varies from breed to breed: Arabians tend toward the horizontal; thoroughbreds have more slope. Extremes of either conformation can limit the horse. If he has flat quarters, he may have trouble bringing his hind legs up under his body, which will put him at a disadvantage in collected work and in sports such as jumping. Quarters that drop off sharply, on the other hand, tend to be weak because the angle between the ilium and the femur is wide open. Just as a vertical shoulder limits the stride in the forehand, steep quarters limit the stride in back.

A deep, wide chest is a plus: It gives the horse's lungs more room and so increases his stamina. Judge depth from the side. Ideally, the distance from the elbow to the withers should more or less equal the distance from the elbow to the fetlock —in other words, the horse's chest is as deep as his legs are long. Judge width from the front; you should be able to see the ribs springing out past the shoulders. Although a shallow-chested horse or a narrow, slab-sided one won't necessarily have soundness problems because of his flaw, and may be perfectly adequate in many events, his endurance will suffer, since his intake of oxygen will be limited. You should make allowances for that when you plan the kind of work he'll be doing.

2. Legs

The way the horse's legs are built determines how, and how well, they move the horse forward and distribute his weight. Deviations can lead to soundness problems, but there's one caveat to keep in mind. If you have an adult horse that has a conformational flaw but is working well all the same, chances are he'll continue to do so as long as his work level and type of work remain the same. The times to be most concerned about conformation-related leg problems are when you bring a young horse into training and when you decide to increase the amount or change the kind of work an older horse is doing.

FRONT LEGS

In the front legs, alignment is the key. When the bones are lined up correctly, the legs travel straight, and stress is distributed evenly through them. Viewed from the side, a line drawn through the center of the leg should drop plumb from the elbow to the fetlock. If you extend this line to the ground, it should graze the heel on the way.

Straightness is no less important when you view the horse from the front. The shoulders should be well muscled, set well apart so that the legs below clear each other easily as the horse moves, and a plumb line from the point of the shoulder to the ground should neatly bisect the leg. When the limbs are closer together at the ground than they are at the shoulder, the horse tends to overload the outside of the hoof and the outside surfaces of the joints. If the feet are set wider apart than the shoulders, the inside is stressed. The result can be sidebone, ringbone, osselets, or other problems on the affected side. Knock knees, bow legs, and bench knees (in which the cannon is set to the outside, so that the knee seems to bulge in on the inside) have similar effects, but the stress is concentrated at the knee.

THE SET OF THE FORELEGS

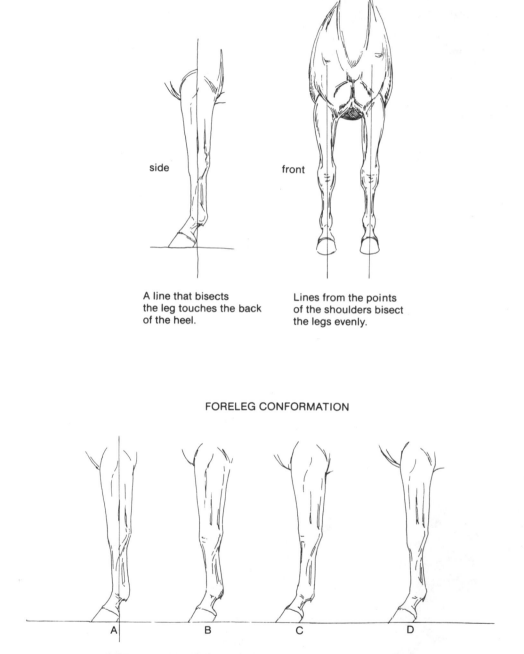

side

A line that bisects
the leg touches the back
of the heel.

front

Lines from the points
of the shoulders bisect
the legs evenly.

FORELEG CONFORMATION

A   B   C   D

(A) Correctly set foreleg; (B) over at the knee, or knee-sprung; (C) back at
the knee, or calf-kneed; (D) tied in below the knee.

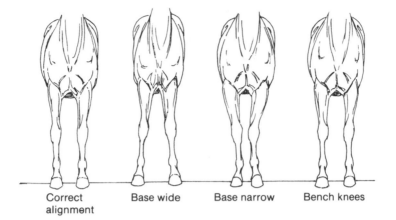

Correct   Base wide   Base narrow   Bench knees
alignment

Often horses whose legs aren't parallel toe in or toe out. A pigeon-toed horse will paddle—instead of traveling straight ahead, his feet will arc to the outside before returning to land in front of him. A horse who toes out will wing—his feet will arc to the inside. These are inefficient ways of going, of course, but sometimes they lead to more serious trouble. A horse that stands with his feet close together and also wings will be likely to interfere, for example.

At one time it was thought that corrective trimming and shoeing could solve most such problems. For example, a horse who stands with his feet close together tends to wear down the outside wall of his foot more than the inside, so that the foot appears to be unbalanced. By trimming the inside wall to match, the feet can be forced to stand farther apart and appear level. But if the narrow stance stems from the horse's build, it may be better to leave it alone—the correction can force bones out of alignment and lead to worse trouble. A safer course may be to watch carefully for signs of trouble and reduce the horse's workload the minute they appear. If the horse tends to interfere, be sure he's wearing protective boots any time he's worked or turned out.

The angle between the pastern and the ground varies from breed to breed, with Arabians tending to have more slope than quarter horses and thoroughbreds. Fifty degrees is a good average. When the pasterns slope too much—say, more than

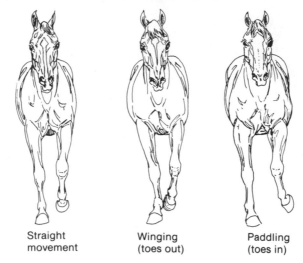

| Straight movement | Winging (toes out) | Paddling (toes in) |

forty-five degrees—the horse is more likely to strain the ligaments and tendons at the back of the leg, and he may be prone to sesamoid trouble. You'll want to avoid situations in which the leg muscles may get fatigued and let the fetlock down too far.

Upright pasterns—steeper than fifty-five degrees—are also troublemakers. In this conformation, the fetlock is an inefficient shock absorber, and bone surfaces are crunched together at every step. Horses with upright pasterns often develop ringbone, navicular disease, and similar bone problems. It may help to go easy on work such as jumping, which puts extra stress on the front legs, and teach the horse to lighten the load in front by traveling in a more collected frame. There are pads on the market that claim to reduce shock when put on under the shoes; while these claims have yet to be proved, you might want to give the pads a try. Keeping the horse in pads year-round is a bad idea, though, because they tend to hold moisture in the foot, so it becomes too soft and doesn't hold shoes well.

One thing you shouldn't do is try to correct the pastern angle by shoeing. The bones of the pastern and the foot should line up straight, so the angle of the hoof wall should match the angle of the pastern. If you try to decrease the angle (by

(A) Ideal, (B) too upright, and (C) too sloping. Note the "coon foot" in (C)—
the angle of the hoof wall is steeper than the angle of the pastern.

trimming the heels and letting the toe grow out) or increase it (by growing out the heel and trimming the toe) you can throw the bones out of alignment and produce all sorts of unnatural stresses in the foot. You may end up with more problems than if you'd left the natural angle alone.

The joints of the legs are prime sites for breakdowns, both because of their functions and because of their construction. If you view your horse's ankles from the side, for example, you can guess their function easily. They're shock absorbers, sinking under the load when the horse puts his weight on the foot and springing back when the weight comes off. And like the feet, the fetlock joints are superbly designed for their job.

Two major bones meet at an angle at the fetlock: the cannon bone and the pastern bone, or first phalanx. The lower edge of the cannon bears a ridge about a fourth of an inch high, running from front to back. It fits like the tip of a screwdriver into a groove on the upper surface of the pastern bone, so the joint slides freely front to back but can't move side to side. Two small bones tucked against the joint at the back, the proximal sesamoids, lend support.

The main support for the joint, however, comes from the ligaments and tendons that bind it together. At the sides, short, tough straps, the collateral ligaments, limit movement. The

THE FETLOCK JOINT

Bones of the lower leg

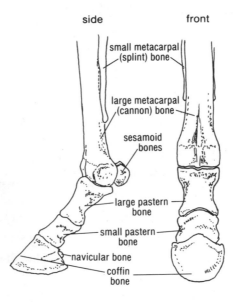

side   front

- small metacarpal (splint) bone
- large metacarpal (cannon) bone
- sesamoid bones
- large pastern bone
- small pastern bone
- navicular bone
- coffin bone

Structures of the fetlock

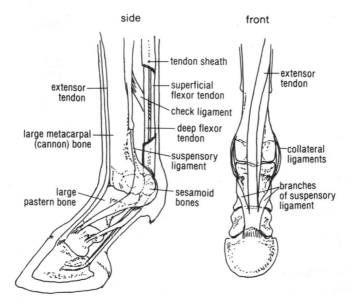

side   front

- tendon sheath
- superficial flexor tendon
- check ligament
- deep flexor tendon
- suspensory ligament
- sesamoid bones
- extensor tendon
- large metacarpal (cannon) bone
- large pastern bone
- extensor tendon
- collateral ligaments
- branches of suspensory ligament

common extensor tendon runs down the leg to cross the fetlock at the front. At the back, the suspensory ligament, which starts behind the knee, divides just above the joint to anchor each of the two sesamoids; the branches then wrap around to the front and join the extensor tendon. Two major tendons also help support the back of the fetlock: the deep and superficial flexors.

In contrast to the foot, which is encased in a heavy layer of horn, the fetlock is virtually unprotected—not even a cushion of fat stands between it and the outside world. This is because it's a working joint with a wide range of movement, and protection would just get in the way. The pastern is normally at a fifty-degree angle to the ground, but when the horse lands from a jump or gallops at top speed, that angle may close to twenty degrees, stretching the tendons and ligaments at the back like elastic straps and compressing cartilage at the front of the joint. When the foot leaves the ground in the next phase of the stride, the bands recoil and draw it up under the horse's body.

Considering the enormous force that the fetlock is asked to absorb, it's not surprising that things occasionally go awry. The horse puts his foot down on uneven ground, yanks the collateral ligaments, and the result is a sprain. Or stress on the joint prompts windpuffs to develop; they are a sign of stress but in themselves are no cause for alarm unless the ankle is hot or the horse is sore.

LUMPS AND BUMPS AT THE FETLOCK

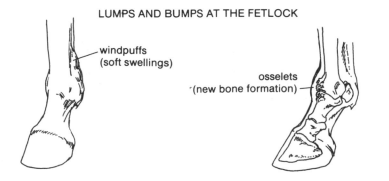

windpuffs
(soft swellings)

osselets
(new bone formation)

Hard lumps are more serious. Osselets ("little bones") are signs of arthritis at the fetlock—new lumps of bone that form around the joint in response to irritation. As in other forms of arthritis, the joint will be hot, swollen, and sore while the new bone is forming, and the horse should be rested. Once the flare-up is over, though, osselets will cause problems only if they interfere with the working of the joint. Occasionally an osselet at the working surface can be chipped away in surgery, but usually these little bumps remain to cause continual irritation.

Fractures range from mild to disastrous. At one end of the scale are chips that break off from either the cannon or the pastern bone at the front of the joint, where it compresses under weight. If the chip works its way into the joint, it can cause trouble, but often these little pieces can be removed in surgery. This has become considerably easier since techniques of arthroscopic surgery have become widespread. Rather than opening up the whole joint, the surgeon makes two tiny incisions—one for a fiberoptic viewing scope, the other for miniature surgical instruments. The result is less trauma and a faster recovery time for the horse.

At the other end of the scale are major fractures often linked to the work the horse does—the slab fracture of the cannon bone caused when the horse rounds a curve at high speed and loads his joint unevenly, for example. When a reining horse or a barrel racer is asked to pivot sharply on his hind legs, the screwdriverlike ridge on the cannon can act like a real screwdriver, twisting in its groove with such force that it shatters the pastern bone. Piecing this type of fracture together with bone screws is tricky because the ridge and groove must line up perfectly for the joint to work.

Sesamoiditis involves both hard and soft tissues—the ligaments and the sesamoid bones at the back of the joint. When the ligaments are stretched too far, they may begin to tear free from the bones. Calcium deposits form at the torn fibers, and the structure is weakened and chronically inflamed. Rest

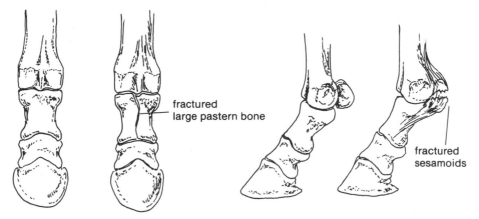

fractured
large pastern bone

fractured
sesamoids

in leg wraps or even a cast will often give the ligaments a chance to heal. But if the force is great enough, the ligament will break the bone as it tears away. A small chip broken off the top can often be removed surgically; a chip off the bottom is harder to reach but may heal naturally if the horse gets six months of stall rest in a cast. If the bone shatters completely, the horse probably can't be brought back to working soundness. The joint can be surgically fused, however, so the horse will be sound enough for breeding and a life in the pasture.

Stress at the back of the fetlock can also lead to problems with the flexor tendons of the leg. Tendonitis is inflammation of the sheaths around the tendon; the cure is rest. More serious are bowed tendons, in which the tendon fibers themselves are torn. Even after the injury has healed, scarring in the tendon may leave the horse with a permanent bulge, or bow, at the back of the leg. It indicates a weakness that may restrict the horse from performing in the hardest equine sports, such as racing, but probably won't limit him in less strenuous work.

The horse's knee is subject to troubles of its own, and here again conformation plays a role. The knee is a hinge, opening and closing the angle between his lower leg and his upper leg. But it's probably the most complicated hinge you'll ever see— no fewer than eight bones, stacked in two layers, make up the joint. There are two reasons for the complex structure: The many small bones and the cartilage packed between them help the knee to absorb shock, and the double layer allows the horse to fold his legs more tightly than he could with a simple joint (just as a string of beads bends easily around a curve).

Like the fetlock, the knee bends in one direction only, and like that joint has stiff collateral ligaments that prevent it from wobbling off to one side. The major flexor and extensor tendons of the leg bend and straighten it, but the lower leg is prevented from swinging forward past the vertical by the lower row of carpal bones (numbers one through four—or three in some horses, because the innermost bone of the row is on its way to becoming vestigial and often isn't present). These bones, which range from pea- to walnut-size, are wedge-shaped, wider in front than in back. When the horse bends his knee, the upper row of bones slides back across the lower row easily. When the leg straightens, they slide forward again, but the wedges stop their progress at the vertical point.

THE BONES OF THE KNEE

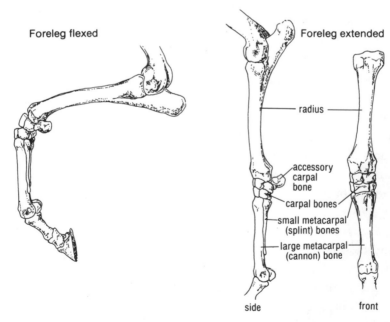

Foreleg flexed

Foreleg extended

radius

accessory
carpal
bone

carpal bones

small metacarpal
(splint) bones

large metacarpal
(cannon) bone

side

front

The tiny bones take a terrific pounding with every stride—worse in sports such as jumping, where they take the full force of landing. Yet because of their shapes and the way they fit together, they handle the weight easily. The critical factor in knee breakdowns isn't weight so much as angle: Any time the leg doesn't meet the ground vertically, the knee is at risk. A horse who lands from a jump onto uneven or sloping ground can tear ligaments at one side of the knee, where they are stretched, and even chip the bones on the other side, where they are compressed more than nature intended.

A horse that is over at the knee—the knee seems to be flexed forward a bit over the lower leg—puts a little extra stress on the sesamoids and tendons at the back of the leg. Two related problems are tied-in knees, in which the joint itself is straight but the tendons at the back of the cannon nip in close, so that the joint hangs over them; and cut-out knees, in which the cannon is set back and the knee protrudes in front. Many horses have one or the other of these flaws and never have a problem, so trainers often find a horse's limit by proceeding with work and then backing off at the first sign of soreness in the knee or tendons. A horse with calf knees may be in more serious trouble. In this conformation, the knee seems almost to be bent slightly back, so that the lower leg extends forward from it. Every time the horse takes a step, he puts pressure on the wedge-shaped fronts of the carpal bones and tugs the ligaments at the back of the knee. Chip fractures are common; you'd do well to avoid high-speed and strenuous work with a calf-kneed horse.

High-speed work is especially risky when it's coupled with fatigue, as it is in a race. At slow speeds and when the horse is fresh, the leg retracts to meet the ground vertically as it takes the horse's weight. At high speeds, there may not be time for full retraction, and tired muscles and tendons won't be as quick to perform as fresh ones. The foot meets the ground slightly ahead of the horse, and as the horse's weight

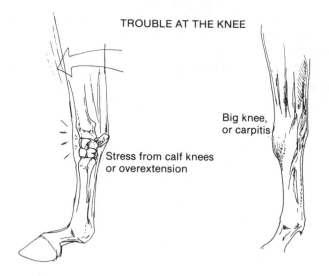

Stress from calf knees
or overextension

Big knee,
or carpitis

moves forward onto the leg, the wedge-shaped fronts of the carpal bones are compressed with enormous force. Thus knee fractures are among the most common racing injuries. Fortunately, many aren't serious. Small chips can be surgically removed and larger breaks fixed with bone screws, so about three-fourths of the horses that suffer these injuries return to full work in about six months.

Horses who do lighter work may not break their knees, but they still get knee troubles. Like the fetlock, the knee is relatively unprotected—armor would just get in the way of bending. And because it's often sticking out in an exposed position —when the horse bends his legs to lie down or get up, or when he folds them to go over a jump, for example—it gets some hard knocks. If the knocks come hard or often enough, the various membranes that enclose the knee joint will start to secrete extra synovial fluid. Pretty soon they stretch, and you see a puffy bulge at the joint—a big knee. Like windpuffs and similar soft-tissue swellings, a big knee can be brought down with leg wraps and anti-inflammatory drugs, but it may return any time the knee is stressed again.

In itself, a big knee is no more than a blemish. But a serious blow or repeated injury can lead to chronic inflammation in the bones and ligaments, a condition that's loosely called carpitis. If the horse isn't rested so that the inflammation can subside, the cartilage in the joint may wear away and new bone may start to grow in response to irritation. And as with other forms of arthritis, if the new bone interferes with the working of the joint, the horse will be continually sore.

HIND LEGS

Many of the rules covering the lines and angles of the front legs hold true for the hind legs as well, but there are differences. From the side, a plumb line from the point of the buttock to the ground should graze the back of the hock and travel down the back of the cannon to the fetlock, finishing about three inches behind the hoof. The pastern angle in the hind legs is usually steeper than the angle in the front legs, perhaps fifty-five degrees on the average, since the hind legs do less weight carrying and more driving. The line from the hock to the stifle should run at an angle, too; while straight hind legs are fashionable in halter classes, they're also prone to weak hocks and locking stifles. This area should also be well muscled, with the muscles tapering gradually to the hock.

LINES AND ANGLES OF THE HIND LEG

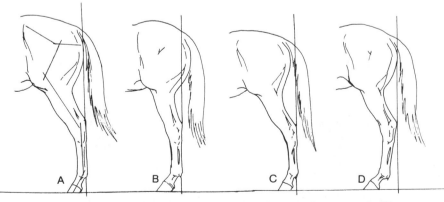

(A) Correct, with back of leg and hock in line with point of buttock; (B) angles too straight; (C) leg set behind the vertical; (D) sickle hocks.

When they nip in abruptly below the stifle, the leg is less powerful.

A hind leg that trails out behind the horse is also a poor power producer; one that stands too far under his body is under extra stress. This second fault often goes hand in hand with one or more defects in the hock. Sickle hocks, for example, are sharply angled, so that the cannon runs forward toward the ground rather than plumb. You can spot other hock defects from behind the horse. Here as in the front limbs, straightness is the key—a plumb line from the point of buttock to the ground should bisect the limb. Bow legs put the hocks outside the line; cow hocks fall inside it. Cow-hocked horses often toe out behind, as well, and because their hind feet don't travel a straight path they may interfere. But all three hock flaws can make the horse predisposed toward curbs, spavins, and other hock problems, and you should take that into account when you plan the horse's work. The greatest trouble will come in sports that force the horse to throw his weight onto his hind legs or pivot on them—western reining, for example—but he may also have problems with collected work. If you let him travel in a more relaxed, hunter-type frame, you'll put the least stress possible on his hocks.

The hock is part of the horse's driving mechanism, flexing when he brings his hind legs up under his body and sinks his

HIND LEG ALIGNMENT

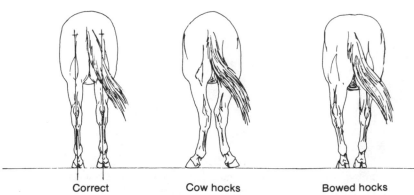

Correct   Cow hocks   Bowed hocks

weight onto them, extending to propel him forward. Perhaps because it carries less weight than the joints of the front legs, fractures (apart from the occasional chip) are less often a problem. But the hock is a complicated joint, and wear and tear take their toll on it.

The main bones leading into the hock are the cannon and the two splint bones, from the lower leg, and the tibia, from above. Between them is an assembly of six bones that not only allow the joint to flex and extend smoothly but also absorb shock between the larger bones. Two disk-shaped bones, the

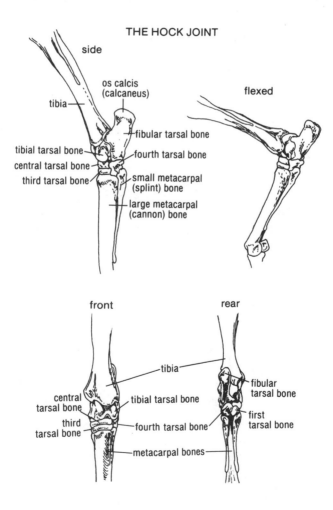

THE HOCK JOINT

side

os calcis
(calcaneus)

flexed

tibia

fibular tarsal bone

tibial tarsal bone

fourth tarsal bone

central tarsal bone

third tarsal bone

small metacarpal
(splint) bone

large metacarpal
(cannon) bone

front

rear

tibia

fibular
tarsal bone

central
tarsal bone

tibial tarsal bone

third
tarsal bone

fourth tarsal bone

first
tarsal bone

metacarpal bones

third and central tarsals, rest flat on the top of the cannon. They're flanked by other small bones—the first and second tarsals, fused together, to the inside, and the fourth tarsal, to the outside. With thick cartilage pads between them, these bones are the chief shock absorbers.

Above them are two larger bones, the fibular and tibial tarsals. The fibular juts up behind to form the calcaneus, or the point of the hock; the major flexor tendons of the hind leg run over and around it. If the joint should ever try to bend backward, this bone would stop it cold. The tibial, in front of the tarsal, is squat and rounded with a deep grove through the middle. A ridge at the end of the tibia fits into this cartilage-coated groove and slides back and forth in it when the hock flexes. As in the fetlock, the groove-and-ridge construction is coupled with strong collateral ligaments to prevent sideways movement. Another major ligament, the plantar, runs from the point of the hock to the top of the cannon, acting as a brace against overflexion.

Nearly every structure in this assembly is subject to stress and damage of one form or another. Thoroughpins are soft swellings in what should be a hollow between the point of the hock and the main part of the joint. They're caused by extra fluid in the sheaths of the tendons that cross this area. Bog spavin is a term for soft swelling at the front and sides; this time, fluid in the joint capsule is the culprit. Fluid can also collect in the sac that covers the top of the fibular tarsal, producing a soft, rounded bulb—a capped hock. All of these soft swellings are signs of stress: thoroughpins arise when the tendons are strained; bog spavin, when the joint is compressed or wrenched; capped hock, when the horse bangs the point of the hock while lying down or trying to kick. The horse may be lame when the injury is fresh. Later, a jellylike bulge may remain as a permanent blemish, but such residual swelling rarely causes trouble.

Soft swellings can be warning signs of unacceptable stress levels, though. And firmer lumps are clear signs of trouble.

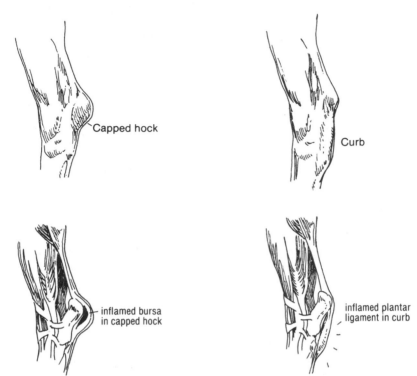

Capped hock

Curb

inflamed bursa
in capped hock

inflamed plantar
ligament in curb

If the plantar ligament is overstretched and tears, the horse will likely be lame. After the injury heals, lameness will subside and he'll sport a curb, a resilient lump of scar tissue below the point of the hock. (If you're checking a horse for an old curb, don't confuse this blemish with the top of the splint bone, which in some horses can be quite prominent. A curb isn't soft, but it gives under pressure, and it's higher than the top of the bone.) As with bowed tendons, whether a curb creates a permanent weakness in the ligament depends on how much scar tissue there is.

Continual strain and inflammation at the hock can set off the same kind of degenerative arthritis that afflicts other joints. Cartilage wears away, and new bone growth usually appears at the front of the joint, where the small shock-absorbing bones are compressed and rub against each other. The hard lumps that emerge here are called bone spavins or jack spavins. Sometimes a horse carries a spavin or two without problem, but often the inflammation turns out to be chronic and progressive. In these cases veterinarians often advise that the horse keep right on working, with the help of anti-inflammatory drugs, because nature has its own way of solving the problem. As irritation continues, more bone is produced, and the small bones eventually fuse. At that point (which may be a year from the onset of lameness) they can no longer rub against each other, so the pain and inflammation stop. The hock has lost some of its shock absorbing ability, but it still functions.

With a shorter range of motion than the hock and less risk from concussion than the joints of the lower leg, the stifle is less subject to arthritis and degeneration. (The same is true of the shoulder and hip joints.) When things go wrong, it's usually the result of injury—the horse falls or catches the joint on a fence rail during a jump. These injuries can be serious, but they're not very common. Still, some peculiarities of design leave the stifle open to problems uniquely its own.

The stifle is the meeting point of the major bones of the upper leg, the tibia and the femur. A third bone gets involved —the fibula, which in the horse is a thin vestigial remnant— but it plays no significant role in the working of the leg. This

SPAVIN

 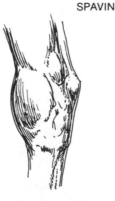  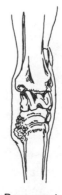

Normal hock   Bog spavin   Normal hock   Bone spavin
(side view)   (front view)

is another ridge-and-grove joint, with a ridge on the upper end of the tibia fitting into a groove on the lower end of the femur. On either side of the groove are two thick cartilage pads, the menisci; ligaments bind the bones together.

What makes the stifle different from other joints is a construction at its front, where the femur sends out two rounded projections. In the groove between them is the patella—the horse's kneecap. This bone, slightly cupped and bearing a vertical ridge on its inner surface, is attached to the tendon of the quadriceps muscle above, to ligaments that run to the femur at the side, and to ligaments that hook up with the tibia below. The entire setup helps extend the joint—when the horse wants to open the angle between femur and tibia, he contracts the quadriceps; the patella slides up in the groove, and the tibia is drawn forward. It also acts as a brake against overflexion, preventing the two bones from folding together entirely under the horse's weight. And when the horse is at rest, the patella construction serves a special function: It helps him remain standing with no muscular effort at all. When the horse relaxes his leg muscles in a standing position, the bulges at the end of the femur drop forward and are caught as if in a sling by the ligaments that join the patella to the tibia. The

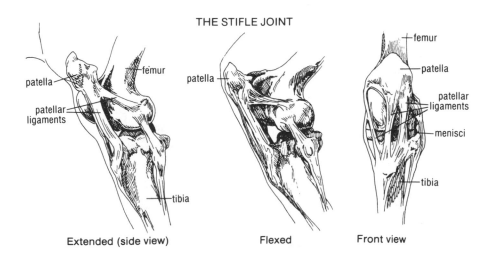

THE STIFLE JOINT

Extended (side view)   Flexed   Front view

patella is held firmly in place, and the stifle is locked in an open position. It won't budge until the horse decides to move.

Two problems—loose stifles and locking, or catching, stifles —stem from malfunctions in the patella-sling apparatus and often go hand in hand. In the first, weak muscles and loose ligaments leave the sling slack, so that instead of running smoothly up and down its groove to draw the tibia forward, the patella jerks along ineffectually. The result is less forward impulsion in the horse's stride—he can't draw his legs up under his body as far as he could otherwise—and a wobbly, uncoordinated gait. Usually the problem is fixed simply by getting the horse in shape, so the muscles perform as they should.

Weak muscles also contribute to locking stifles. In this condition, the joint slips into its locked-open position unbidden— muscles let the femur down when they shouldn't, and it slips under the patellar ligaments. The horse suddenly can't move the leg forward, and he may hop for a stride or two until the femur pops free. When this happens repeatedly, the cartilage on the working surface of the patella can start to degenerate, and arthritis gets started in the joint. Whether it stems from a locking stifle or an injury, arthritis in the stifle is difficult to treat and usually progressive, and it often leaves the horse disabled. So a locking stifle is worth correcting. And if feeble muscles are the only cause of the problem, conditioning will do the trick. Or the problem can be solved by surgery, in which the vet cuts the innermost of the two main patellar ligaments. This leaves the mechanism intact for flexing and extending the leg but does away with the sling. The horse may lose some of the impulsion in his stride, but he'll still be able to work. Of course, he'll have to sleep lying down.

Such an operation may be necessary, because in many cases muscle tone is only part of the problem. Locking stifles are one of dozens of lameness problems that are closely tied to the horse's basic conformation. In this context, the more open the angle between tibia and femur—that is, the straighter the leg —the greater the danger of locking stifles.

3. Feet

The heart of the foot is a joint between three bones: the spade-shaped coffin bone, the boxy small pastern above it, and the small navicular or distal sesamoid bone. The navicular is tucked behind the other bones in such a way that weight coming down through the small pastern bone is deflected through it to the heel, as well as through the coffin bone to the toe. The bones move very little—tight ligaments ensure that they do not—but the joint gives just enough under pressure to absorb some of the shock of landing. Two major tendons are anchored in the foot and help flex and straighten it: The extensor runs down the front of the leg and attaches at the most prominent point of the coffin bone, and the deep digital flexor passes behind the joint to the bottom of the coffin bone. Where it crosses the navicular, its fibers fan out to help support that bone.

THE FOOT

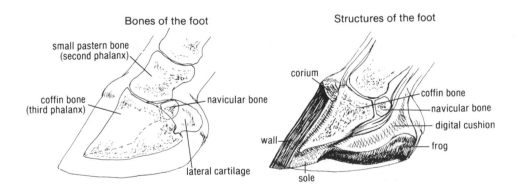

Bones of the foot

small pastern bone
(second phalanx)

coffin bone
(third phalanx)

navicular bone

lateral cartilage

Structures of the foot

corium

coffin bone

navicular bone

digital cushion

wall

frog

sole

If the bones and tendons of the foot had no more protection than your toes and fingers, they wouldn't carry the horse a hundred yards—his weight and rough terrain would pound them to shreds. But they're protected by what amounts to a suit of tough, resilient armor, the hoof, which has a consistency more or less like vinyl. It's formed of protein, not unlike the material of your fingernails but many layers thick. Hoof wall grows down in tiny tubules from the corium, a band of tissue at the top of the hoof; it can take up to a year for material formed at the top to reach ground level, where it will be worn away or trimmed off by the farrier. The sole is formed from a layer of similar tissue beneath the coffin bone.

Design makes the hoof a shock absorber. The hoof wall, about three-eighths of an inch thick at the toe, narrows gradually to a thickness of about a quarter of an inch at the heels. There it turns inward on each side to form the bars of the sole, two ridges that run back toward the toe. This construction allows the hoof to expand slightly under pressure. The

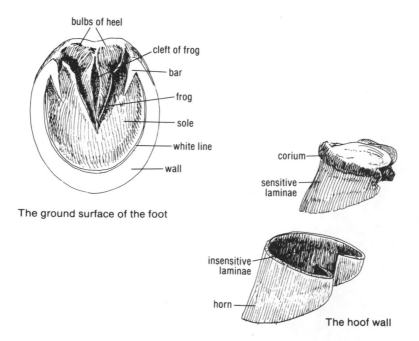

bulbs of heel

cleft of frog

bar

frog

sole

white line

wall

The ground surface of the foot

corium

sensitive laminae

insensitive laminae

horn

The hoof wall

sole itself doesn't touch the ground—it's slightly concave, so it deflects force out to the walls—but some of the weight is borne by the frog, a V-shaped pad that divides the sole in two.

Within the heel is another structure that helps absorb concussion, the digital cushion. This is a pad of elastic fiber, well padded with fat and held in place between the bones and the heels by two broad wings of cartilage that run back from the coffin bone. When weight comes down on the foot, the cushion flattens, pushing the cartilage wings out. Because the hoof wall is thinner at the sides than the front, it expands a bit, too. Pressure on the digital cushion also helps circulation; when the pad is squeezed, blood is forced up out of the foot into the veins of the legs.

A good front foot is rounded, just slightly longer than wide, with wide heels and well-developed frog and bars. Hind feet are more oval in shape. Narrow feet may be poor shock absorbers, and they may tend to develop concussion-related soundness problems. In narrow feet, too, the sole is often too concave, with deep crevices around the frog that set the horse up for thrush, a fungal infection in the frog and sole. The thrush organisms thrive in the dark crevices of the frog (the better if the crevices are also damp) and cause the dead outer tissues to degenerate; pretty soon, you notice a foul, rotting odor and see a dark discharge in the crevices. Thrush is rarely serious, but it can weaken the sole. Thoroughly cleaning the crevices and painting on a copper sulfate or iodine solution usually works; keeping the feet and stall clean are the best preventives.

The problems caused by narrow feet will be compounded if you let the walls grow too long between shoeings, so that the frog is raised off the ground and is no longer forced to expand by contact with it. On the other hand, platter feet—with widely flaring walls and flat soles—are easily bruised. Shoeing with protective pads may help, and the farrier should be careful not to trim the sole or the frog too thin.

Feet that are too small in proportion to the horse's body

don't fare well because they have too little area over which to disperse shock. Such feet were fashionable among thoroughbred and quarter horse breeders for years, and while the trend is away from this now, there are still plenty of horses around that sport them. If your horse does, you need to give extra consideration to the effects of concussion. Avoid work on hard ground and sports that increase concussion, such as jumping. Shock-absorbing pads may also help.

THE HOOF WALL

Another common defect is a thin hoof wall. This is a headache for you and your farrier because the hoof won't hold shoes well and because the thin wall will give the farrier little space in which to drive nails. To avoid the damage that can be done when a shoe pulls loose, you'll need to be extra careful about having the horse shod on schedule. Also be sure that the horse is getting all the nutrients he needs and is free of parasites, because poor nutrition can affect wall quality. Exercise is a help rather than a hindrance in this problem, because it tends to stimulate wall growth.

Moisture gives the hoof its ability to expand and spring back without cracking; without it, the wall would shatter under the horse's weight. The hoof wall is about twenty-five percent water. The sole is a bit softer than the wall because it has more water; the frog is softer than the sole for the same reason. The moisture is supplied by circulation inside the foot, so the wall gets progressively drier closer to the surface. Its outermost layer is made up of horny scales that help keep moisture in, but some is always evaporating. This is all to the good—if the foot became too moist, it would be soft, and it wouldn't bear up under weight. A lot of hoof wall problems can be traced to the moisture level in the horn itself—the hoof is too moist, so it's soft and won't hold shoes; or it's too dry, so it cracks. The softness is most apt to develop if the horse lives in a damp environment or is always shod with pads over his soles, because the pads tend to hold moisture. The dryness can stem from work in dry, sandy soil that scrubs off the outer protective layer of the hoof, but it can also result from lack of exercise which reduces circulation (and therefore moisture) in the foot. Nutrition plays a role in hoof condition, but it's not well understood. Despite the fact that a lot of feed supplements on the market claim to promote good hoof growth, no one knows for sure which nutrients help. There is some evidence that adding biotin (available as a supplement) to the feed helps healthy foot growth. But many vets think an adequate basic diet is all a horse needs.

Cracks in the wall usually run vertically. They can be inconsequential (the little hairline ones called sand cracks) or serious, if they are deep enough to reach the sensitive tissues underneath or extend up to the coronary band. Poor shoeing that leaves the hoof out of balance, so that it bears more weight at one point than another, is often to blame in more serious cracks, which can pop up suddenly at the toes, quarters (sides), or heels. Damage to the coronary band—from a cut or a blow—can produce a flaw in the wall that can be a potential starting point for a crack.

If a crack looks as if it might develop into something serious, you need a farrier quickly—farriers have a number of techniques to keep a crack from spreading. The farrier may cut away the lower edge of the wall below a small crack, so that the wall won't bear weight and expand there, and rasp a notch in the wall above the crack to stop its spread. A more serious crack may be sealed with screws, laces, or epoxy plastics.

If a crack involves the sensitive structures, you need a vet— there's risk of infection entering the foot. When infection takes hold, through a crack in the wall or sole or through a puncture, the result is usually an abscess. The foot will be hot and extremely sore. The treatment is usually to pare open the sole at the infected area to let the abscess drain, and then follow up with epsom salts soaks and medicated packing. Sometimes antibiotics are prescribed to keep the infection from spreading deeper into the foot and leg.

The sole can be bruised when the horse steps on a stone or some other foreign object. He may be sore for a few minutes or a few days, but weeks later you'll see a red or darkened mark on the sole as the damaged area grows out. Most bruises don't need treatment. But corns, which are bruises at the point where the wall turns in to form the bars, are another story because they're usually a sign of poor shoeing. Corns turn up when the shoes are too narrow or too short for the feet or when the heels have been trimmed too short; in either case, there's too much pressure on the sensitive tissues below the heels. The horse should be shod extra wide in the heels or perhaps have bar shoes, which have an extra band across the heel, to take pressure off the area while the corns grow out.

Unbalanced shoeing contributes to a host of other problems that develop in the heels, although it's not always the sole cause of these ills. In sheared heels, one heel has been left longer than the other, so that it takes more weight and gradually gets pushed up and away from its partner. If the horse is shod so that his weight doesn't fall naturally on his heels and frog (or if some other problem makes him keep his weight off his heels), the heels can gradually become contracted—narrow, close together, and underdeveloped. Both conditions can be corrected by a good farrier, but it takes time because new hoof growth is slow.

Concentric rings in the wall may be superficial, or they may stem from more serious problems. So-called fever rings show up a few weeks after the horse has been sick; they simply show that the coronary corium wasn't operating up to speed at that point and are no cause for concern. Many such rings may indicate that the horse is chronically ill or in poor condition. And a foot that's marked by many deep grooves that dip down at the toe is showing signs of chronic laminitis, one of the most serious problems that can affect the foot.

LAMINITIS

Laminitis affects the union of the hoof wall and the underlying bone. Normally, bone and hoof are kept firmly locked together with an ingenious device: A layer of tissue over the surface of the coffin bone sends out thousands of tiny hairlike projections, the sensitive laminae. They mesh like interlocking fingers with similar projections on the inner side of the hoof wall, the insensitive laminae. The resulting bond is so strong that it can withstand thousands of pounds of pressure.

In laminitis, the laminar tissues become inflamed. In serious cases, the bones can separate from the wall entirely and even punch through the sole; at this point the horse is said to have foundered. Researchers are still trying to figure out exactly what goes on in laminitis. The mechanism at work is thought to be a disturbance in the horse's circulation, perhaps caused by toxins in his system. Part of the reaction to the toxins seems to be that capillaries in the feet constrict, so that blood flow to the laminae is cut off.

Laminitis has many triggers: hard work on a hard surface, a heavy feed of rich grain, putting the horse up when he's hot and sweating from a workout. Whatever sets it off, it's an emergency condition that needs immediate veterinary attention, and you should memorize the signs: Because his toes hurt, the horse may lift first one foot and then the other to relieve the pressure. In a severe case, he tries to keep his weight on his heels, and he stands with his feet planted out in front of his body. He's unwilling to move, and shuffles when he does, and he has great difficulty turning corners. Often (but not always) there's heat and increased pulse in the foot.

If you detect laminitis in its early stages, walk the horse to keep circulation moving to the feet as much as possible—just a few steps each minute is enough—until the vet arrives. The vet will probably administer vasodilating drugs to restore circulation and painkillers to make the horse more comfortable.

If the coffin bone has pulled fully away from the wall, the recovery may take a long time, up to a year. But even horses that have foundered severely can recover—there are radical corrective shoeing techniques that force new hoof wall to grow down in alignment with the new position of the coffin bone. And several research centers are working to develop a vaccine that may prevent laminitis.

Much milder forms of laminar separation can occur. They may stem from an inflammation (perhaps so mild that you were unaware of it) or from unbalanced shoeing. "Seedy toe" is the name for this condition when it turns up at the toe, but it can occur anywhere. When you tap the hoof wall over the affected area, it may sound hollow, and as the defect grows down you may see it in the white line between wall and sole as a blurry, thickened area or even as bloody spots. The danger here is that infection will work its way up behind the wall, so treatment usually involves medicated packing and a wide shoe to protect the area.

BONE PROBLEMS

Problems in the bones of the foot range from fractures (most common in the coffin bone) to a host of degenerative conditions, some more serious than others. One of the less disastrous is sidebone, in which the lateral cartilages gradually calcify in response to repeated stress on the foot. The horse may or may not be lame while the calcification is going on. Once it's complete, he probably won't be unless the new bone formation is enough to restrict his foot (which it may be if his feet are small or narrow to begin with) or unless the sidebone later fractures.

Unfortunately, sidebone often turns up with other, more serious conditions. One of the most common—and baffling—of these is navicular disease, a degeneration of the tiny navicular bone and inflammation of the joint sac around it and of the deep flexor tendon that runs across it. Navicular disease is most common in the front feet, and it usually hits both, although one foot may be more affected than the other. It's slow and progressive, starting out with intermittent lameness (worst after work) or perhaps just a shortened stride. The horse's heels hurt, so he tries to trot along on his toes. At rest, he may rest one foot or the other, pointing it forward and cocking the heel off the ground.

But any heel lameness—sidebone, sheared heels—can cause these signs. And X rays aren't always conclusive. The navicular bone is tucked away behind the other bones, and it's hard to get a clear shot at it. The disease may start out affecting only the soft tissues. And as horses get older, most show some changes in the navicular area without becoming lame. So the vet usually diagnoses navicular disease by ruling out all other possible causes of lameness. It's not a welcome diagnosis—the condition is permanent and usually gets worse.

The exact cause isn't known, and there may be many factors at work. One theory has it that the disease starts with tiny clots that form in the blood vessels that serve the area, blocking circulation, and researchers have had some success treating it with anticoagulants. But the drugs themselves are risky, so the treatment isn't widely used. Mild cases are usually managed with corrective shoeing and anti-inflammatory drugs, such as phenylbutazone. In more severe cases, the horse may have an operation called a neurectomy, in which the nerves to the area are cut so he can't feel pain (as long as the nerves to the toe are left intact, he'll still know where to put his feet). But both treatments are aimed at making the horse more comfortable—they do nothing to stop the disease.

Because the joints between the bones of the foot move so little, the tendons and ligaments around them rarely rupture. But strain on these structures leads to other problems. As the tendons and ligaments are stretched and pulled, they yank against the membranes that surround the bones. The bones respond to this irritation with lumps of new growth—ringbone. Ringbone can be low, when the bumps pop up in the foot itself, on the upper end of the coffin bone, or the lower end of the second phalanx (the small pastern bone); or high, about an inch above the coronary band, on the upper end of the second phalanx or the lower end of the first phalanx (the long pastern bone that runs up to the fetlock). High ringbone is easier to spot, since the lumps can be felt beneath the skin, but either way the diagnosis usually requires X rays.

Typically the horse will be quite sore while the new growth is forming—the active phase of the disease. If it's caught early enough, rest and anti-inflammatory drugs help keep inflammation to a minimum. Some veterinarians even recommend that the leg be put in a cast to keep it entirely immobilized. Whether or not the horse continues to be lame after the lumps have formed depends on their location. If they're between the bones or near ligaments and tendons, they may interfere with the working of the joint and be a chronic source of trouble. If not, chances are that the horse may just sport a blemish that will cause no problem. Occasionally lumps that interfere can be surgically removed, but those deep in the foot are usually inaccessible.

Certain conformation flaws—small feet, narrow feet, upright pasterns—seem to contribute to this and other concussion-related foot problems, so such defects are warning signs that may lead you to limit your horse's performance. But although conformation-related soundness problems are real and serious, they are far from being the most common or even the most serious causes of lameness. One survey of racetrack veterinarians, for example, indicated that conformation accounted for as little as a fourth of lamenesses; by far the majority were caused by exercise stress and failure to prepare the horse properly for it. Even perfect conformation, then, is no guarantee: For the most part, your horse's soundness depends on the work you ask him to do and the basic care you give him.

CHAPTER IV

Fuel, Control, and Protection:

THE RESPIRATORY, DIGESTIVE, CIRCULATORY, AND NERVOUS SYSTEMS AND THE SKIN

Imagine that the car of your dreams is parked in your driveway—Porsche, Rolls, whatever it may be. It's yours. There's just one catch: The gas tank is empty, so the car is useless.

A horse is no different. No matter how perfectly his bones and muscles are put together, he can't perform unless his fuel lines—the respiratory and digestive systems, which provide oxygen and nutrients, and the circulatory system, which delivers them—are up to par. The horse needs something else, too, if he's to function properly: control lines that coordinate all the working parts and keep them running smoothly. The nervous system does this.

Just as much as the mechanical systems of bone and muscle, these fuel and control lines are open to attack. Disease can strike any part of your horse's body. Its effects can range from short-term and limited to long-term and lethal; its causes, from allergies and mechanical breakdowns to invasions of parasites, bacteria, and viruses.

Fortunately, the horse has a built-in line of defense—the immune system—that helps him battle many contagious diseases and leave the field unscathed. By giving him the right care, you can help him in the fight against these and other conditions, and you can even make it possible for him to avoid some of the most serious diseases altogether.

1. The Respiratory System

In a sense, the horse's respiratory system works as both carburetor and exhaust system, drawing in the oxygen that's essential to metabolism and ridding the blood of the waste carbon dioxide produced by the body cells' fuel burning. In design and function, however, it's at once more capable and complex than the mechanical systems of a car—it not only draws air in but cleans it, warms it, and humidifies it as well.

Air enters through the nostrils, which are normally relaxed but can flare wide to increase their intake when the need for more oxygen arises through exercise or excitement. Just inside the nostrils are hairs that trap dust and other particles, and a fine network of tiny blood vessels located near the surface of the skin. These blood vessels have a special job—warming the

THE RESPIRATORY SYSTEM

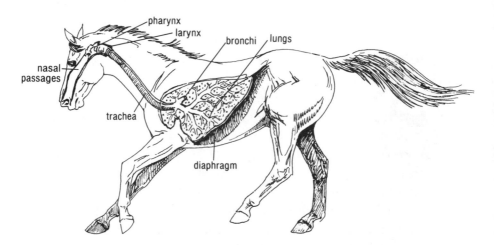

air on its way in—and the blood flow through them increases during cold weather. Meanwhile, moisture secreted by the surface of the nasal passages mingles with the air.

At the end of the nasal passages, the air crosses the pharynx. This area is a sort of highway junction, where the routes of the respiratory and digestive systems meet, and a complex group of valves makes sure that food on its way to the stomach doesn't take a wrong turn here and wind up in the lungs.

The main working parts of this valve system are the epiglottis, a triangular flap of tissue stiffened by cartilage that at rest lies on the floor of the pharynx, and the cartilages of the larynx, a short, stiff tube that joins the pharynx to the windpipe. These cartilages are the two arytenoids, which form an inverted V at the opening of the windpipe, and the cricoid and thyroid cartilages behind them. When the horse swallows, his tongue pushes back, forcing the epiglottis up over the opening of the windpipe and drawing the arytenoids together to seal the airway. Food passes over the seal and down the esophagus, which runs behind the windpipe. The larynx has another function, too: With its vocal folds—tissue-covered ligaments that run vertically on either side of the opening—it permits the horse to whinny.

The windpipe itself, a good three feet long and two inches or so in diameter, is made of elastic tissue. Rings of cartilage stiffen it and hold it open for the free passage of air, and a mucous lining lubricates it. But if you could look down this tube, it would seem to be lined with velvet. Throughout the lining are special cells with hairlike projections called cilia that constantly beat upward to carry specks of dust and other impurities out of the windpipe.

Near its end the windpipe begins to divide, first into two main bronchi that lead to the right and left lungs, then into several secondary bronchi, and finally into many bronchioles. These progressively smaller tubes—like the windpipe, made of elastic tissue and lined with mucus-secreting and ciliated cells—lead ultimately to the air sacs, or alveoli, of the lungs. Dozens of these tiny sacs cluster at the end of each bronchiole; there are millions in each lung. This is where the basic respiratory function takes place: Oxygen hops across the membranes of the air sacs and through the thin walls of tiny blood vessels that surround them, while carbon dioxide makes the trip in reverse.

The design of the lungs ensures the maximum surface area for this exchange. The air sacs are tucked neatly into the horse's ribcage, but if the stretchy tissue that forms their thin walls were spread out flat, it would cover more than a fourth of a football field. The oxygen–carbon dioxide exchange follows a natural law: Molecules of any substance tend to move from areas of high concentration to areas of low concentration. The blood that circulates around the air sacs has just completed a trip through the body; its oxygen levels are depleted, but it's loaded with carbon dioxide. Molecules of these gases slip through the membranes in an attempt to restore balance. A second factor in the exchange is hemoglobin, a component of red blood cells, which draws oxygen toward itself.

The horse doesn't think about breathing any more than you do; the process is prompted unconsciously, by the blood's oxygen levels. A small group of specialized cells in the brain monitors these levels continuously and senses when they begin to drop. Their job is essential: The horse can go for days without water and weeks without food, but he can live only three minutes without oxygen. Long before oxygen becomes so scarce that body cells would be damaged, though, the brain sends a signal to the diaphragm, a sheetlike muscle that starts at the top of the horse's last rib and runs diagonally down to the bottom of his sixth rib, dividing the chest from the abdomen. The diaphragm tenses and draws back, while other muscles expand the ribcage. The chest cavity grows larger, air pressure inside it drops, and fresh air rushes in to balance the pressure. Exhalation is simply relaxation—the diaphragm and the other muscles relax, and the stretchy tissue of the lungs springs back, forcing air out.

At rest, a horse will go through these steps twelve to sixteen times a minute. As his need for oxygen increases, his breathing will become faster and deeper. A galloping horse breathes in rhythm with his stride, inhaling as his hind legs come under his body to propel him forward and exhaling as his weight is caught by the lead foreleg. The rhythm makes breathing easier because during the stride, the weight of the abdomen first shifts back, giving the diaphragm free play, and then shifts forward, helping exhalation.

During hard exercise a horse will also flare his nostrils and straighten his airway by stretching out his chin in an effort to draw in the maximum amount of air—as much as ten gallons —with each breath. Obviously a horse asked to work in a collected frame, with his chin tucked in, would have difficulty doing this. But other factors also affect the amount of air a horse draws in. A narrow or shallow chest will simply hold less air than a deep, wide one, and a horse that's built this way will run out of oxygen quickly and will be able to do less distance and endurance work. A fat horse breathes less easily than a fit one because his diaphragm has to work against his weight.

Excitement, illness, heat, and humidity also affect breathing. While a horse who needs oxygen will breathe more deeply, an overheated horse will take rapid, shallow breaths in an attempt to replace the air in his lungs the second it is warmed. Panting plays an important part in the horse's temperature control mechanism because the air also draws off heat along with carbon dioxide from the blood. Other variations in breathing patterns may be keys to trouble. For example, inhalation and exhalation are normally of equal length. If the horse draws long, labored breaths, he may have an obstruction in his airway. If the exhalation is long and forced, he may have emphysema. A cough is an attempt to expel some irritant that has gotten into the respiratory tract. The horse draws a breath and then closes his larynx, allowing pressure to build up as the diaphragm relaxes. When he opens the larynx, the pressure forces out the air in a rush, with the characteristic sound.

RESPIRATORY DISEASES

Not surprisingly, your horse can catch a cold, just as you do, although it's unlikely that he'll catch your cold or you his. The infectious agents that cause colds in humans generally aren't at home in horses, and the same holds true the other way around. The effects are much the same, though: The horse has a runny nose and perhaps a cough and a sore throat. He may lose his appetite and run a fever.

How serious the situation is depends on what infectious agent is at work and how extensive the infection is—how deep it travels into the respiratory tract. For a mild cold, the vet may simply prescribe rest; for a more serious case, where fever is present and the infection looks as if it may be taking hold deep in the airways, he may prescribe antibiotics. Antibiotics aren't effective against viruses, which cause many colds and actually enter living cells (where the drug can't reach) to destroy them from within. But antibiotics may prevent secondary bacterial infections from starting up in the already embattled respiratory tract.

One of the most common—and serious—bacterial infections in the upper tract is strangles, caused by Streptococcus equii. These bacteria can enter through the nose or mouth and then infect the lymph nodes of the pharynx. White blood cells rush to the scene to fight the infection; as they die and pile up, abscesses form and restrict the horse's breathing. Treatment often involves opening and draining the abscesses. But vets are divided on the wisdom of giving antibiotics as long as the infection is localized and the abscesses can be reached—it's possible that the drug will kill only the weaker bacteria, leaving resistant ones free to multiply and spread without competition. And if they move to lymph nodes in a new site, such as the chest, abscesses may not be accessible. This condition is called bastard strangles.

Farms often suffer repeated outbreaks of strangles because the bacteria can live for up to a year, in a dormant state, outside the horse. Most horses who've had the disease once build up considerable immunity, though, and usually can fight it off the second time. Still, a second bout with strangles is possible and has dangers of its own. The circulating antibodies will attach to the new bacteria, or antigens, in an attempt to destroy them. But the attempt isn't successful. Instead, the new antibody-antigen combination is more harmful to the horse than the bacteria alone would have been. It causes a condition called purpura hemorrhagica, in which blood and lymph vessels are damaged. The vaccines currently available for strangles aren't a hundred percent effective, but they might be worth a try if you live in an area with a high incidence of the disease.

Two common viruses that cause coldlike symptoms in horses are equine herpes I, which causes rhinopneumonitis, and the equine influenza virus. Like similar agents, they're transmitted from horse to horse by coughs and sneezes, so horses who travel around to shows or move from barn to barn are easy prey for them. Most horses who contract one of these diseases bounce back within a week, during which time they should rest in a well-ventilated stall away from other horses, who might catch the disease from them. But their defenses will be below par for another three weeks or so. You should think twice before you stress a horse by returning to his regular work schedule (rhino in particular can lie dormant for weeks and then flare up again when the horse is stressed) or by taking him off to a show where he could be exposed to new viruses and bacteria (or expose other horses to lingering viruses in his system). Depending on the severity of the case, a total rest time of four to six weeks may be in order.

Both diseases can be prevented by vaccinations, and the shots are good investments because in certain circumstances rhino and flu can be extremely dangerous. In pregnant mares, the rhino virus can cross the placenta to the foal, whose immune system is too immature to deal with it. The foal dies, and the mare aborts. And when rhino strikes a horse for the second time, she may suffer an odd and potentially lethal side effect, much as purpura hemorrhagica can follow strangles. Antibodies formed by the immune system to deal with the viruses in the first attack are still circulating; when fresh antigens enter, they attach to their surfaces in an attempt to knock them out. But instead, the new combination damages nerve fibers, and the horse can be paralyzed.

Flu is dangerous chiefly because the virus that causes it can set up housekeeping in the lungs as well as in the upper respiratory tract, setting off a case of viral pneumonia. Pneumonia is the term for any inflammation in the lungs, whether it's caused by viruses, bacteria, fungi, or some corrosive substance the horse manages to inhale. Occasionally parasites in the lungs (roundworms in young horses, lungworms in horses of any age) weaken the horse's defenses and open the door for pneumonia. Whatever the cause, in response to the irritation the air sacs fill with fluid and debris, and the horse has difficulty breathing. He'll run a fever and seem depressed. The vet, listening to his lungs, will hear gurgling sounds, and when he taps the chest he'll hear a dull thump. If the infection isn't stopped, the horse's lungs may be permanently scarred. Also, lung abscesses and lingering bronchial infections often follow a bout with pneumonia. Less often, but more seriously, bacteria sometimes pass through the air-sac walls to the bloodstream, producing a raging and potentially fatal system-wide infection. The best way to avoid these threats is to treat respiratory infections early, before full-blown pneumonia develops.

Pneumonia is often complex and difficult to treat because once one type gets started, there's danger of secondary infections joining in. To stop the infection, the vet has to find out what agent is at work; the usual way of doing this is with a transtracheal wash. The vet inserts a needle directly into the windpipe and then slides a length of fine plastic tubing through it and down toward the lungs. Next he sends a minute amount of sterile fluid through the tube, lets it mix with the bronchial secretions, and draws it back out. The fluid goes to a lab to be cultured; if certain bacteria or fungi are at work, the vet can prescribe the appropriate antibiotic for them.

Pleurisy is an inflammation between the double membranes that separate the lungs from the chest wall. Because the condition is very painful for the horse, he'll take rapid, shallow breaths, and he'll probably be feverish and depressed. Pleurisy can follow another respiratory infection, or it can arrive on its own, often when a wound penetrates the chest wall. It's serious—fluid buildup in the membranes limits the horse's breathing and can force a lung to collapse—but, fortunately, not too common. To treat it, the vet may draw off fluid from the chest, culture it, and prescribe antibiotics and anti-inflammatory drugs.

Respiratory infections and inflammations of all kinds seem to be most common when horses are kept in a damp or poorly ventilated barn, so keeping your barn open and airy is a good preventive measure. As long as direct drafts are kept off the horse, this applies even in winter—"a cold barn is a healthy barn" is an old horseman's saying.

There can be mechanical failures in the respiratory tract, too. One of the most common is roaring, or laryngeal hemiplegia. The horse makes a roaring or whistling noise with each breath, especially during work, because one of the two arytenoid cartilages that form an inverted V at the back of his throat no longer moves out of the way to allow air through. The nerve governing the muscles that draw it back has been damaged; through lack of use, the muscles gradually atrophy. It's not clear what causes the nerve damage, but it may be that the sheer length of these nerves (which run all the way up from the chest) makes them prone to breakdowns.

The problem is most common in the left side. To diagnose it and judge the extent of the paralysis, the vet may peer into the throat with a fiberoptic endoscope. A severe case can limit the horse's intake of air, and roarers are disqualified in certain show categories, such as the hunter division. If you don't show in one of these divisions and if your horse's case doesn't affect his performance in the work you do with him, you may choose to live with the condition. But most cases can be fixed by surgery. There are two operations. The first, for mild cases, is done under local anesthetic. The vet takes out a fold of the mucus lining behind the vocal cord, and the scar tissue that forms as a result stiffens the throat and helps support the arytenoid. The second operation is usually done under general anesthetic. The vet puts a suture in the place of the atrophied muscle and draws it tight, so that it holds up the arytenoid permanently.

Similar noises can be caused by cysts, polyps, and other growths in the airway; nearly all these can be surgically removed. A far more serious breakdown, however, can occur in the lungs: heaves, or chronic obstructive pulmonary disease.

Heaves can stem from any of three conditions. The first two are similar—chronic bronchitis and chronic bronchiolitis. The walls of the passages leading to the lungs are inflamed and produce quantities of thick, sticky mucus, so they're narrowed. The third condition is similar to emphysema in humans— mucus collects in the air sacs of the lungs, and they rupture or simply lose their elasticity, so they no longer spring back into shape to force air out of the lungs.

In all three versions, the external signs are much the same. The horse can still inhale—muscles widen the airways and expand the lungs. But in exhalation, the muscles relax, and that's where trouble comes in. As the airways become narrower, or as more and more air sacs are damaged, the horse has to make a forced, muscular effort to exhale. You may see his abdomen push up at the end of each exhalation, and a horse that has the condition for a while may actually have a roll of muscle along his abdomen. The horse coughs and breathes heavily; as the disease progresses, he becomes less and less able to work because his lungs can't draw enough oxygen or clean the blood of waste gases efficiently.

There are many possible causes for heaves—damage from a lingering infection (particularly likely when the horse is put back to work too quickly); an allergy to dust, mold in hay, or some other environmental irritant; even a reaction to certain elements in some pasture grass. There may well be other causes, too, that researchers haven't turned up yet. Not knowing the precise cause makes any disease difficult to treat, and heaves is no exception. In acute flare-ups, corticosteroids are sometimes used to reduce inflammation, along with bronchial dilators to relax spasms in the passages. Other drugs will thin the mucus in the airways, so the horse can cough it up. But these treatments just ease symptoms; they don't get at the root of the problem. Heaves has classically been considered an irreversible condition that will progressively get worse.

However, that may not be true for all cases. If damage to the air sacs is extensive, it's likely that the horse won't get better; but if the cause is chronic bronchitis or bronchiolitis, removing the irritating agent should do the job. There are two catches. First, it's extremely difficult for a vet to distinguish between the three conditions, because the signs are so similar. Second, it's equally hard to pin down the agent at work. If the horse has an allergy, for example, he may wheeze immediately on exposure or six hours later, during which time he's been exposed to countless other possible agents.

Still, there are steps that can be taken. A transtracheal wash can determine if bacteria are at work. Even if there is damage in the air sacs, removing irritants such as dust and mold can slow the progress of the disease, so putting the horse in a well-ventilated, dust-free environment—turnout, if possible, or stabling on mats—often does wonders. The horse can go on a pelleted complete ration to remove the risk of dust from hay. And researchers at several major veterinary clinics have had some success with allergy testing and desensitization shots, using techniques more or less like those used in human medicine. All of these measures have the greatest chance of success if the disease is found early, before damage is extensive.

Horses in high-stress sports such as racing suffer another rather mysterious ailment—pulmonary bleeding. Some estimates put the percentage of racehorses who are bleeders at seventy-five or higher, but this is little more than a guess because mild cases often go undetected. The cause is equally unclear; one theory suggests that in many cases, high blood pressure brought on by hard exercise ruptures the thin-walled vessels in the lungs. If the bleeding is heavy, blood will be exhaled and seen at the nose or mouth, and if it's extensive enough it will limit the horse's performance. Many racetrack bleeders, however, have no problem with less strenuous sports such as jumping. A diuretic drug called furosemide (Lasix) is often used to lower blood pressure, and it helps. However, this drug is restricted or banned at many tracks because it masks other drugs so they can't be detected.

2. The Digestive System

A tube more than one hundred feet long makes up most of the digestive system that provides your horse with the energy and nutrients he needs. Along its path from mouth to tail, this tube, called the alimentary canal, bends and turns and takes different shapes to perform different functions. Glands and other accessory equipment located near it facilitate the process, but the tube itself is much the same throughout—walled with double or triple layers of smooth muscle, lined with mucous membrane, well serviced by blood vessels.

This system differs from your digestive tract in many small ways, but there are two major differences in its concept. First, horses are herbivores: They'd have trouble digesting the kind of omnivorous diet you prefer, but they are more adept at processing plant matter than you are. Second, the horse's system is designed for almost continuous nibbling and digestion, rather than occasional large meals. These differences will determine what and how you feed your horse.

The process begins at the mouth. If you hold out your hand and offer your horse a carrot, he'll probably reach for it with his lips, not his teeth. The flexible lips are equally adept at gathering up blades of grass, shreds of hay, and mouthfuls of grain. The front incisors are slicers; they can chop off a piece of the carrot or a clump of grass. On the other hand, the molars and premolars that march down the horse's cheek are grinders—their flat surfaces could not break down meat fibers, but they can mash vegetable matter to a pulp.

This step is essential, especially with hard-shelled grains. The surfaces of the teeth wear down with continuous grinding, but for most of the horse's life more tooth continues to push up from the gum. A horse that is "long in the tooth" is an old one whose grinding hasn't kept pace with this growth. Serious problems can develop if the teeth wear unevenly, though—if the grinders' flat surfaces don't meet, much of the food the horse takes in will pass through undigested.

THE DIGESTIVE SYSTEM

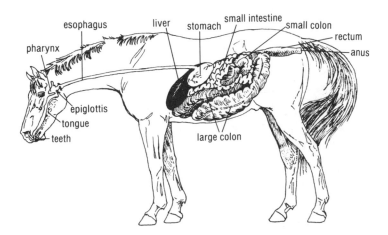

Digestion gets under way as the horse chews. Saliva, produced by glands in the horse's upper neck and at the sides of his face, travels through ducts to the mouth. It moistens the food and, because it contains ptyalin and other enzymes, begins to change starch into sugars. When the carrot you gave your horse leaves the mouth, it's a sort of carrot mash virtually unrecognizable save for its color.

The tongue pushes this mash back toward the pharynx, and as it leaves the mouth, a soft flap of tissue on the roof of the mouth, the soft palate, rises up to block the nasal passages. (This seal also prevents the horse from breathing through his mouth.) At the same time, the epiglottis and the arytenoid cartilages seal the windpipe, so the food has no choice but to start down the esophagus. This section of the digestive tube, nearly five feet long, is walled with a double layer of muscles that contract in rhythmic waves to push the food along.

At the end of the esophagus the food reaches the stomach, a U-shaped holding tank that receives whatever the horse eats and sends it along to the small intestine in a comparatively steady flow. For his body size, the horse has a fairly small stomach; the capacity is about four gallons, but the stomach functions best with between two and three gallons inside. That makes large meals difficult, if not dangerous. Overloading the stomach leads to trouble because once in, food can't leave the way it came—the entrance valve, called the cardiac orifice, is locked by a powerful sphincter muscle, and a fold of the stomach lining covers its inner surface. In addition, the wave-like contractions of the esophagus can't be reversed. The horse can't vomit; whatever enters the stomach, even a poison, must continue through the digestive system.

When food enters, the stomach's walls are stretched, and that prompts two events. Three layers of muscle in the wall—running lengthways, crossways, and diagonally around the stomach sack—begin to contract in waves, squeezing and mixing the contents. And the walls begin to secrete hydrochloric acid and enzymes that start to break down complex sugars and proteins. Gradually the food is pushed toward the back of the stomach, where it passes through the pyloric valve and into the small intestine. Water tends to pass through the stomach rapidly; solid food takes longer.

The small intestine can hold three times as much food as the stomach—it's some seventy feet long and can stretch to three or four inches in diameter. Only the first few feet have a definite shape; this section, the duodenum, is a fixed arch. The rest of the small intestine is coiled any which way into the abdominal cavity, filling the space near the horse's left flank and held in place by a sheetlike membrane called the mesentery.

At the duodenum, ducts from the pancreas and the liver (which in the horse weighs anywhere from ten to twenty pounds) discharge pancreatic juice and bile. These secretions neutralize the acids arriving from the stomach, and they contain enzymes that break down starch and proteins into their components—glucose and amino acids. The horse doesn't have a gall bladder, which in humans serves as a holding tank for bile. Because his system is designed for frequent small meals, bile trickles into the small intestine continuously.

As food moves on through the small intestine, nutrients are absorbed into the bloodstream by hairlike projections, the villi, that line the walls. Each of these tiny projections is served by capillaries and a lymph duct. By the time the food reaches the start of the large intestine, gastric secretions have made it mostly liquid, and much of the starch and protein in it has been broken down and absorbed.

A major exception is cellulose—the material that makes up the cell walls of plants—and since the horse is a vegetarian, there is likely to be a sizable amount of this. Cellulose is broken down in the cecum, the first four feet or so of the large intestine, which contains a small army of cellulose-digesting bacteria. The bacteria break down the cellulose (the process is very much like fermentation), take what they need, and the horse gets the rest.

Beyond the cecum, the food travels through the four large folds of the large colon, which is in all about twelve feet long and perhaps ten inches in diameter, and the narrower but equally long small colon. Any remaining nutrients are absorbed here, along with the fluids the horse consumed and those he secreted during digestion. The remaining solids pass through the rectum and out. Start to finish, the trip through the digestive system can take as long as eighteen hours, but most of the time is spent in the various sections of the large intestine.

The design of the digestive system suggests some feeding practices. First, meals should be small and frequent to avoid overloading the stomach. Be particularly careful to avoid feeding a big meal right before exercise, for two reasons—the demands of muscles will call blood away from the digestive tract, so digestion won't proceed on schedule, and the horse's distended stomach may push against his diaphragm, making breathing difficult. Second, because water passes through the stomach quickly, it makes sense to water the horse before, rather than after, a meal—otherwise water may wash food through the stomach too quickly. (It's all right, though, to let the horse sip water with his meal.) Third, because the stomach functions best when it's about two-thirds full, it makes sense to offer hay before grain. Grain is rich and concentrated; you'd never give your horse enough to fill his stomach. If hay is given first, the horse will fill up partially on it, and the stomach will be functioning when the richer grain arrives.

COLIC AND OTHER DIGESTIVE PROBLEMS

Colic is the number one killer of horses, but not all cases are serious. The term covers almost any sort of digestive pain, caused by any of a number of agents. At the onset, it's difficult to tell what kind of colic is at work—all forms produce similar symptoms. The horse may refuse food and pass less manure. He may paw at the ground and turn to look or nip at his abdomen. If the pain is more severe, he may get up and down restlessly, roll, or sit on his haunches like a dog. His pulse and respiration will increase. His flanks may seem bloated, and depending on exactly what's happening inside, gut noises may be louder or softer than normal or entirely absent. The more severe the pain and the longer the attack goes on, the greater the risk of the horse going into shock. In shock, his temperature will drop and, as his circulation pools in the vital organs, mucous membranes will take on a dusky hue.

The most common cause of colic is probably intestinal parasites, and parasites account for some of the more serious forms of colic. In their immature stages, strongyles, or bloodworms, travel to the mesentery, the membrane that holds the small intestine to the abdominal wall and through which the major blood vessels supplying the intestine pass. The strongyles can damage the blood vessels, or, by creating irritation, set off waves of contractions. As a result, a section of the intestine twists or telescopes into itself, and blood supply to it is cut off. Twists can also occur in the large intestine. In both cases the tissues will die if the problem isn't corrected quickly. But emergency surgery can often straighten out the tangle, and if the tissue damage isn't too extensive the surgeons can remove the dead sections.

In young horses, a heavy infestation of roundworms can sometimes block the small intestine. Blockages can also be caused by bits of indigestible matter that the horse has eaten, or by food consumed when the horse hasn't been getting enough fluids, especially if the feed is coarse and stemmy or if the horse's teeth are in poor condition so he can't grind his food properly. Some blockages respond to drug treatment—painkillers and antispasmodics, along with cathartics such as mineral oil and antifermetic drugs that cut down the production of intestinal gas. More serious ones may require surgery.

Feed or feeding practices are often to blame for gas colic, which is usually (but not always) less serious than a twisted or blocked intestine. Gorging, a sudden change of feed, too much rich spring grass, or damp, moldy, or spoiled feed can all set off colic. Horses that graze or are fed off sandy ground may pick up bits of sand that irritate the digestive tract. If the horse is fed right before or just after work, his intestines will be undersupplied with blood and he may colic. The same may happen if he's allowed to drink his fill of water right after work. Usually the indigestion type of colic responds to drugs, and surgery isn't necessary.

Time is of the essence in treating colic, however, because of the risk that the horse will go into shock and die. The risk increases dramatically if the attack lasts six hours or more. You should call the vet immediately; until he comes, hand-walk the horse so that he won't injure himself by thrashing around. An anti-inflammatory such as phenylbutazone or Banamine and a tranquilizer such as acepromazine will make the horse more comfortable, but even if you have these drugs on hand there are two reasons why you should hold off administering them until the vet arrives.

First, some veterinary research has shown that because of their method of action, anti-inflammatories like Banamine are double-edged swords. When a colicky horse goes into shock, it is probably because his intestines produce excess toxins that leak into his system through damaged intestine walls. The toxins disrupt circulation and metabolism, so that peripheral tissues are deprived and die. Part of the effect is to stimulate the production of hormones called prostaglandins, which are associated with pain, fever, and inflammation. Banamine and similar drugs suppress prostaglandins and help control the situation. But the drugs don't affect other hormones and harmful enzymes, which continue to leak into the blood, damaging the system. Oversuppression of prostaglandins can have harmful effects—some of these hormones help protect the lining of the gut, for example—so the drug dosage should be carefully calculated.

The second reason to delay drug treatment is that the drugs

will make it more difficult for the vet to assess the problem and decide if surgery is required. Even so, it may be difficult for the vet to determine what's causing the problem. Usually, if the attack lasts eight hours or more, he'll want to perform exploratory surgery.

Parasites can cause other digestive problems, such as diarrhea, as well as systemic problems, such as fluid loss and anemia. Because the immature forms of many parasites migrate through the horse's body, they can cause a lot of trouble, ranging from irritation at the rectum caused by pinworm larvae (the horse may rub his tail raw to relieve the itching), to colic caused by strongyle larvae blocking the mesenteric artery, to abscesses and peritonitis (a generalized inflammation of the abdominal cavity) caused by other strongyle larvae that have carried bacteria with them through the wall of the gut. Bots, the larvae of flies, attach to the stomach wall and cause ulcers. Onchocerca migrate to the ligamentum nuchae, the main ligament of the neck, and coil up inside it, creating small nodules. All horses probably have some of these parasites and others, such as tapeworms. They can be killed off with chemical dewormers, but different dewormers affect different parasites, and many leave the immature forms unscathed.

The best way to keep the problem in check is through a preventive program of regular deworming and good pasture management. Coupled with careful controls on the quality and quantity of the horse's feed, such a program will avert most cases of colic and go a long way toward keeping the horse in general good health. Specific dewormers and feeding schedules are taken up in later chapters.

Horses also get a number of bacterial infections in the intestinal tract, of which the most vicious is probably caused by salmonella bacteria. This infection is highly contagious—the bacteria are passed from an infected horse in manure and can live a long time in damp and dirty surroundings until they're accidentally injested by another horse. Salmonella infections are also difficult to treat because, like viruses, the bacteria manage to get inside body cells where most drugs can't reach them. While the horse is under treatment for this or any intestinal infection, it's important that he have enough water, because fluid loss can be a problem. He can have his usual ration if he's hungry for it. Good stable hygiene—including periodic paddock clean-ups—is the best preventive.

A virulent and often fatal intestinal infection was identified in the eastern Atlantic states in the late 1970s, and researchers traced its cause to rickettsia. Rickettsia are microorganisms that are neither bacteria nor viruses; they cause some human diseases, such as Rocky Mountain spotted fever, that are transmitted by ticks. Further research may lead to better methods of curing or preventing the disease, which is called equine monocytic erlichiosis (EME), or Potomac fever.

Poisoning can produce signs of colic, but depending on the poison at work it may also lead to neurological breakdown or more subtle and gradual problems, such as anemia or liver failure. Occasionally horses eat poison due to negligence on the part of their owners. There have been cases, for example, of horses getting into strychnine-coated grain intended for rats. More often, though, the culprit is a pasture weed. Plants that can poison horses include black nightshade (common throughout the United States); chokecherry, jessamine, torpedo grass, rattleweed, white snakeroot, and yew (mostly in the East and Midwest); and castor bean, crotalaria, death camas, horsetail, fiddleneck, latana, milkvetch, yellow star thistle, senecio, and oleander (mostly in the West). There are others; you should comb your pasture for them. The nearest Cooperative Extension Service office or equine clinic should be able to tell you what plants are native to your area, how to recognize them, and what symptoms they produce.

If you think your horse has been poisoned, you need a vet. Until he arrives concentrate on keeping the horse as calm and quiet as possible; meanwhile, try to find the poison, so the vet will know what course of treatment to follow.

"Choke" is a common equine problem. This isn't choking in the human sense, in which something lodges in the trachea; rather, it's a blockage in the esophagus. It's most likely to occur when a horse bolts his feed or is startled while eating something chunky like an apple, or when his teeth need attention and he can't chew properly. He'll be obviously distressed —breathing rapidly, trying to swallow, saliva and perhaps even food particles dripping from his mouth and nostrils. Choke needs immediate attention because the horse may inhale food or fluid and develop pneumonia as a result. If the block is near the top of the esophagus, the vet may be able to dislodge it manually; if it's farther down, the usual course of action is to insert a tube into the esophagus and either flush the obstacle down or suction it up. Surgery is rarely the answer because the esophagus heals poorly and is prone to infection.

Choke can often be prevented. Cut up treats such as apples and carrots, and take the horse off bulky pelleted feed if that seems to be the cause of the problem. A horse that habitually bolts his feed can usually be slowed down by putting a few large rocks in the bottom of his grain tub, so that he has to eat around the stones.

3. The Circulatory System

Respiration and digestion would be useless if the horse couldn't distribute oxygen and nutrients to every cell of his body, and that's the job of the circulatory system. But circulation does more than this: It carries away wastes, distributes heat throughout the body and helps regulate the horse's temperature, and fights infectious agents that gain entry to the body.

Two subsystems accomplish these feats, the lymphatic system and the cardiovascular system. Lymph is a clear, yellowish fluid that carries some nutrients, especially fats, to the tissues and also plays an important part in clearing the system of wastes and responding to invaders. It begins as excess inter-cellular fluid and circulates throughout the body in a network of ducts. Lymph nodes located along the way trap wandering bacteria, and special cells called phagocytes destroy them. The lymph ducts converge into wider and wider ducts until, near the heart, they join into one main duct, which empties into a major vein.

The bulk of the criculatory work is done by the cardio-vascular system—the heart, arteries, veins, and capillaries and the blood that flows through them. The heart is a four-chambered pump weighing about seven or eight pounds and located between the lungs, in the left half of the horse's chest. Veins bring blood from the body to the upper chamber on the right, the right atrium. As pressure in this chamber builds, it contracts and the blood is forced into the lower chamber, the right ventricle. Pressure here again forces contraction, and the blood is sent out of the heart through the pulmonary artery to the lungs, where it is cleaned of carbon dioxide and replen-ished with oxygen. It returns to the heart through the pul-monary vein, entering the left atrium. Pressure and contraction send it on to the left ventricle, the most muscular of the chambers. When this chamber's walls contract, the blood is pushed into the horse's main artery, the aorta.

One-way valves between the atria, ventricles, and arteries prevent any blood from being forced back the way it came; when enough blood has passed, these valves snap shut. The distinct "dub" of the heartbeat is the sound of the simultaneous closing of valves between the ventricles and the pulmonary and aortic arteries. The softer "lub" of the beat is produced when the valves between the atria and the ventricles close at the same time. At rest, the horse's heart beats thirty to forty times a minute, but the rate is continually adjusted to meet the demands of the body tissues during exercise or other stress.

As the blood moves away from the heart, it passes into narrower and narrower branching arteries and finally into tiny capillaries. The capillaries link the arteries to the veins that will carry the blood back to the heart, and it is through their thin walls that oxygen and nutrients are passed to the cells and waste products picked up. Every cell can't have its own capillary, of course, so much of the exchanging is done through clear fluid that permeates the tissues between the cells.

The blood vessels, especially the arteries, have elastic walls that can dilate and contract to control the flow of blood to various parts of the body. If certain muscles are called into work, the arteries leading to them will open to allow more blood to flow through. In the same way, when the horse is overheated, small arteries and capillaries near the skin dilate, so that more blood will get the benefit of the cooling effects of outside air. Exercise itself aids circulation; as muscles contract, they press on veins, forcing blood to speed back toward the heart. The blood can't move backward through the veins because small one-way valves block its path.

About sixty percent of the blood is a fluid called plasma; the other forty is made up of three types of specialized cells— red cells, white cells, and platelets. A liter of a typical horse's blood has more than eight trillion red cells, nine billion white cells, and three billion platelets. But the warm-blooded breeds —such as thoroughbreds and Arabs—tend to have as much as thirty percent more red blood cells than do cold-blooded horses. This is a key factor in their superior endurance; the red blood cells are the agents that carry oxygen, so a horse with more of them can deliver more oxygen and perform longer aerobically.

Red cells are produced in the bone marrow and stored in the spleen, which releases extra cells when the need arises and also breaks down the used-up red cells. On the average, a red cell lasts about twenty-one weeks. Its chief working component is hemoglobin, which can grab onto molecules of oxygen and hold them until the cell reaches an area of tissue that needs them.

White cells are the disease fighters. There are five types:

lymphocytes and monocytes (produced by the lymph nodes, spleen, and other organs) and neutrophils, eosinophils, and basophils (produced by the bone marrow). The white cells circulate until they encounter some foreign object—perhaps a bacterium or a virus. Then, depending on their type, they may destroy it by surrounding and ingesting it; produce an antibody that will neutralize it; or touch off an inflammatory response that will call other white cells to the scene to perform these functions. Special receptors on the white cells enable them to recognize and thwart specific types of invaders. Part of the response touched off when they encounter a particular type is a signal to the body to produce more of the cells that can fight it. Thus a horse that has been infected by a certain strain of bacteria once will likely be better able to fight it the second time around.

Platelets, which are also formed in the bone marrow, have a different role—they are responsible for blood clotting. When a blood vessel is broken, platelets mass at the site and pile up to form an initial block. Then insoluble strands of a substance called fibrin, formed from protein in the plasma, mesh across the opening, trapping more blood cells and creating a tight seal.

The plasma is a clear, pale yellow fluid—red cells give blood its color. About ninety percent of the plasma is plain water, but some important materials, carried along in solution, form the other ten percent. They include antibodies, hormones, and other essential body proteins. The plasma also carries nutrients broken down in digestion and transports carbon dioxide from the cells to the lungs.

Circulation is the essential link between the other body systems—the bones and muscles, respiratory and digestive tracts. It's also the most readily adaptable of the systems, changing the output, makeup, and pattern of flow of blood on demand. The capabilities of your horse's cardiovascular system play an important role in determining how well he performs as an athlete and bears up under other forms of stress.

Fortunately, there's much you can do to ensure that these capabilities reach their maximum. Cardiovascular work is an important part of conditioning. When the horse's brain senses that the muscles need more oxygen, it orders the lungs to work harder. The respiration rate increases, more air sacs are filled, and more capillaries form around them to collect the oxygen and release carbon dioxide. The heart also works harder and, being a muscle like any other, becomes stronger as a result. A conditioned horse's heart can beat faster for longer periods of time, and it also increases its stroke volume—the amount of blood it pushes out with each beat—by as much as forty percent. The increase in stroke volume means that the horse can work harder without taxing his heart to the limit and that after work he'll recover faster because he's better able to clear wastes and repay the oxygen debt owed to the muscles.

Conditioning has effects throughout the circulatory system. When a horse is in work, his body produces more red blood cells and turns them over faster, clearing out old, fragile cells that are less efficient at carrying oxygen. The spleen, which stores extra red cells for emergency use, lays in more of these cells and releases them more quickly on demand.

New capillaries develop, not only around the air sacs, but also in the muscles, where they release oxygen, and near the skin. The blood vessels just under the skin act like radiators, releasing excess heat produced by the muscles' work, so the fit horse doesn't get as hot as an unfit one. Better blood supply to the skin also means that more nutrients are brought in, so the coat takes on a healthy gleam. Increased blood flow to the feet has similar salutary effects—new hoof horn forms more rapidly and is stronger, healthier, and less likely to dry out.

All these helpful effects make cardiovascular conditioning one of the best forms of preventive medicine around. We'll see how this type of conditioning fits into a general conditioning program in a later chapter.

DISEASES OF THE HEART AND CIRCULATION

Severe heart problems are rare in the horse; hardening of the arteries and sudden heart attacks even more so. But horses are prone to a number of heart and circulatory problems. There are congenital defects, murmurs, and arrhythmias that can spell trouble or not, depending on their type and severity. Sometimes inflammation or damage to heart muscles or valves follows a bout with a respiratory infection. Occasionally, subtle damage to the heart goes undetected until the horse suddenly dies; the most famous example of recent times was the Kentucky Derby winner Swale, who died in 1984 at the height of his career and in apparent full health.

When a horse's heart is failing, fluid may collect in his legs and abdomen (if the failure is on the right side) or in the lungs (if the problem is on the left) because blood backs up in the veins and loses fluid through the vessel walls. He'll tire quickly, and he may cough or lose his appetite. His heart rate may exceed his pulse. But these are extreme signs. A veterinarian who suspects more subtle heart disease may refer the horse to a clinic for detailed diagnostic work, including an electrocardiogram, which measures the electrical activity in the heart muscle, and perhaps cardiac catheterization to measure blood pressure in the heart itself. Rest of a month or more often gives inflamed heart muscle a chance to recover; many arrhythmias are permanently set right with drug treatment.

Fatigue and generalized swelling, or edema, can be a sign of circulation-related problems other than heart disease. For example, damage to blood-vessel walls, shock, and low blood protein levels can all cause fluid to be lost from the blood into the spaces between the body cells. Tiredness can result from an overload of parasites or from anemia, which is a deficiency of red blood cells or their principle ingredient, hemoglobin, which transports oxygen. Anemia produces signs similar to those of respiratory problems—the horse breathes heavily in work, for instance—but an anemic horse will often also have pale gums and eyelids, rather than the usual healthy pink. A blood test can make the determination. The cause may be blood loss from an injury, parasites, or a diet deficient in protein or iron, copper, folic acid, or other vitamins and minerals.

A serious viral infection, equine infectious anemia (EIA), causes red blood cells to form abnormally; the body's immune system then destroys these cells, and the horse becomes anemic. In its acute form, this disease causes high fever and sometimes incoordination and paralysis. Usually the animal dies. Horses can also suffer recurrent bouts with milder forms of EIA and can carry the virus and transmit it without showing symptoms. EIA can be detected with a blood test, the Coggins test, which is usually required when transporting a horse from one state to another.

Horsemen are fond of blaming sluggish performance on anemia and feeding their charges various blood tonics (many are available). In fact, however, anemia of all kinds is fairly rare among horses. If a horse acts tired, chances are he's overmatched—he's been given too much work with too little conditioning to prepare for it.

4. The Nervous System

The lines of control that keep the other systems working in a smooth and coordinated fashion make up the nervous system. The tissues of this system are formed of supersensitive cells adept at transmitting signals from one to another and to bone and muscle. Together, they create a network with a central control panel and two-way communication that allows the horse to respond to any stimulus from outside or inside his body.

The control panel is the central nervous system—the brain and the spinal cord. These structures are the most well protected in the horse's body. Both the brain and the spinal column are wrapped in membranes and encased in bone (the skull and spinal column); the spinal column is further padded by layers of fat and muscle.

Compared to other animals, the horse has a brain that's rather small for his size. What this means in terms of his intelligence isn't clear. Traditionally, equine intelligence has been ranked at about the middle of the scale of domestic animals—smarter than a cow, for example, but not so smart as a dog. Assessing animal intelligence is tricky, though. You may think your horse stupid to panic at the sight of a coiled hose or an empty feed bag waving in the breeze. But horses didn't evolve to live in safe barns. In the wild, the smart horse —and the one that survived—was the one that ran first and asked questions later. The hose might be a snake; the moving feed bag, a predator.

The spinal column is like a massive communications cable, with millions of nerve cells laid in tracks leading to and from the brain. Branch cables serving every part of the body enter and leave it through spaces in between the vertebrae. Most of the branches follow the paths of the arteries. Nerve tracks leading to the brain carry sensory information—for example, a report that a fly is biting the left flank. Those leading away carry commands—swish the tail left to swat the fly. Similar exchanges control the basic body functions, such as breathing, digestion, temperature regulation, and so on. But some simple events (such as the horse's reflex reaction of snatching his foot away when something irritates the fetlock) may never involve the brain; the exchange is handled by the ganglia, secondary nerve centers in the spinal cord.

Closely allied to the nerves are the sensory organs that allow the horse to see, hear, taste, and smell the world around him. Horses have highly developed senses of smell and hearing, as befits an animal that has had to be alert for predators. Much of the hearing talent depends on the ears' ability to swivel individually forward and back, picking up sounds from all quarters. Occasionally a bad case of lop ears (ears that flop to the side) will limit this ability enough to reduce the horse's hearing, but probably not so much that his use for riding will be limited.

A horse's vision is different from yours—better in some ways, worse in others. Because eye problems are fairly common and are certain to limit a horse's use, it's worth understanding how the eye works. The fact that the horse's eyes are placed on the sides of his head at its widest point gives him a visual field of almost 340 degrees, compared to your 108-degree field—only a small segment directly behind him is invisible. Usually each eye sees a separate view, with some overlap in front, and the brain puts the picture together. The horse can concentrate on the area directly in front of him, but it takes some effort on his part, and if his head is up he won't be able to see the ground for about three feet directly in front of him.

The structure of the eye itself gives the horse better night vision than yours but makes it more difficult for him to focus sharply on individual objects. The basic eye structures are the same as yours. An adjustable diaphragm, the iris, controls the amount of light that enters through the clear tissue of the cornea; the light passes through the lens and is focused on the retina at the back of the eye, where special cells (rods and cones) detect it and transmit signals through the optic nerve to the brain. But the horse also has a layer of iridescent cells on the upper part of the back of the eye, and when light is dim they reflect and intensify images, giving the horse better night vision. To keep the glare from being too intense during the day, his iris is designed to block more light than yours. The horse also has some protective structures that you lack— a third eyelid, the membrane nictitans, which can slide across the eye, and a fat-filled cavity behind and above the eye that gives the organ room to move back if it's bumped.

On the other hand, the muscles that change the thickness of the lens to focus images are less well developed than yours. It's thought that the horse compensates with another method:

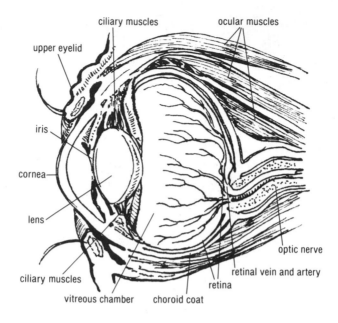

ciliary muscles   ocular muscles

upper eyelid

iris

cornea

lens

ciliary muscles

vitreous chamber   choroid coat   retina   optic nerve   retinal vein and artery

Because his eyeball is not perfectly round, parts of the retina are closer to the lens than others, and by moving his head he can change the angle of his vision to direct the image to a section where it will be focused sharply. In any case, the horse's difficulty in focusing quickly on an object is another explanation for his tendency to shy.

Nerve tissue is the least adaptive of any in the horse's body —essentially, he works with whatever equipment he's issued at birth. Damage heals slowly and often incompletely—sometimes not at all. That makes it doubly important to be alert for neurological problems; while all of them can't be cured, some can be nipped in the bud with surgery or other therapies.

SENSORY PROBLEMS

Horses can develop a serious central nervous system problem that's loosely known as the wobbler syndrome. The spinal cord is involved, and as a result, the horse becomes progressively uncoordinated. Early signs are difficult to distinguish from hind-leg lameness—you notice a mild irregularity of gait. But close examination shows that rather than moving with the limited, painful steps of lameness, the horse simply can't tell where to put his feet: The communications lines between his legs and his brain are interrupted.

So far, three separate causes of the problem have been nailed down. In classic wobbler disease, calcium deposits in the vertebrae narrow the vertebral canal. Big, fast-growing horses seem to be most often affected by this condition, which often strikes when the horse is young, and there may be some connection with diet, perhaps excessive carbohydrates or calcium supplements. The problem can sometimes be fixed surgically, either by fusing vertebrae or by removing sections of bone, depending on its location.

The second cause is a protozoan *EPM* that gets into the spinal cord and destroys nerve tissue, probably by producing toxins. This invader hasn't been fully identified, and no surefire treatment has been developed for it. The condition is considered mildly contagious because it seems to crop up frequently on certain farms; researchers think the horse may be an intermediary host for the protozoan, with another animal also carrying it. Horses of any age can develop this condition, although it seems to be most frequent in younger ones. A number of research programs around the country are working on finding a cure.

The third cause is a mysterious and diffuse degeneration of the spinal cord that seems to affect very young horses. Cells die out all along the cord, and the horse gradually becomes weaker and more uncoordinated. Researchers are divided on what role heredity plays; because all breeds are affected, some think a dietary imbalance or an environmental toxin may be at work. This is another area of current research, but, as with the protozoal form, the outlook for a horse with degenerative spinal cord disease is poor.

Three other neurological disorders go by the common names stringhalt, shivering, and sweeny. In stringhalt, the horse makes an exaggerated snatching motion when he flexes his hock to draw his hind foot off the ground. Stringhalt may affect one or both hind legs and is most evident when the horse has been resting or is turning a corner, and in cold weather. The motion may be barely detectable and intermittent, or it may be so extreme that the horse hits his abdomen with the front of his fetlock. The exact cause is unknown, but the disease seems to stem from degeneration of the nerves that control the hind leg. Stringhalt is considered an unsoundness and usually worsens with time, but a mild case may not prevent the horse from performing well. The working part of the leg that is most affected is the lateral digital extensor tendon, which runs down the leg on the outside. If a section of this tendon is surgically removed, the horse usually shows marked improvement, and such surgical correction is common.

Shivering is not so easily helped. In this condition, the horse snatches his hind leg off the ground and holds it flexed and quivering in the air. The tail also extends and shakes. Often both hind legs are affected; sometimes a front leg is involved. Backing or turning sharply often sets off an attack. Like stringhalt, shivering may be mild or severe, but unlike

In stringhalt, the horse makes an exaggerated snatching motion when he draws his hind leg off the ground.

stringhalt, it has no quick surgical fix. Shivering tends to get worse with time.

Sweeny is a muscular problem with a neurological root; a nerve controlling a muscle is injured, the muscle no longer works, and it gradually atrophies and wastes away. Classically the term sweeny is used for an atrophied shoulder muscle, an injury more common in draft than saddle horses, but it can refer to any wasted muscle. Because the muscle has shrunk, the area appears hollow or flattened. The outlook depends on what caused the damage to the nerve and whether or not it will heal, and the only cure is time. Nerve regrowth is very slow; it may be six months or more before you know whether the horse will regain use of his lost muscle. (It's also possible for muscles to atrophy from simple disuse—when a horse is laid up in a cast, for example—in which case they should gradually return to function as the horse begins to use them again.)

Infectious agents can also attack the nervous system, often with disastrous results. The most common and feared are tetanus and the three strains of equine encephalomyelitis: eastern, western, and Venezuelan. All four can be prevented by vaccination.

Tetanus bacteria are common on farms and can live for years in soil in a dormant state. They may pass right through the horse's intestines without doing harm. The problem comes when the bacteria are trapped away from air, as they would be in a puncture wound. Then they begin to produce toxins that may send the horse into convulsions (usually set off by loud noises) and produce spasms in his muscles. He'll stand with stiff ears and raised tail, with his legs spread in a "sawhorse" stance, and the third eyelid (the nictating membrane) may draw across his eyes. As the disease progresses, he'll be unable to swallow. Administering tetanus antitoxin can sometimes thwart the bacteria if things haven't gone too far, but very often the disease is fatal. Far from being rare, it's actually fairly common, but only among unvaccinated horses.

Equine encephalomyelitis is a viral disease spread by mosquitoes. The eastern and western strains occur in wide areas of the United States; so far, the Venezuelan strain has been confined mostly to the Deep South and Southwest. The disease produces a mixed bag of neurological symptoms, including blindness, staggering, wandering and circling, incoordination, and paralysis. Most horses who get this disease die (the western strain is somewhat less deadly than the other two), and those that survive often suffer permanent damage. There are vaccines against all three types but no universally effective treatment once the horse catches the disease.

Some rarer diseases produce symptoms similar to tetanus or encephalomyelitis. Botulism, like tetanus, is caused by a bacterial toxin, albeit a less common one. In adult horses it produces general muscle weakness and inability to swallow; the horse may lie down and be unwilling to rise. In foals it causes the "shaker foal" syndrome—foals are weak and depressed, don't nurse well, get up and down often, and shake. Some breeding farms have a recurrent problem with botulism and vaccinate against it.

Horses can also get rabies, which can take either the furious or the dumb form. Since this disease is usually spread by the bite of an infected wild animal, vaccination is a good idea in areas that have had outbreaks of rabies among wildlife.

EYE PROBLEMS

Injury and irritation are common causes of blindness in horses, and in many cases the blindness need never have occurred: Prompt treatment could have saved the horse's sight. In injuries, the greatest danger comes from scarring in the cornea, and the longer the inflammation caused by the injury goes on, the greater the amount of scarring. The same is true for inflammations that are set off by dust or pollen and then become infected. If the horse's eye is tearing, the lids swollen, and the mucous membranes reddish, it needs treatment. Antibiotic drops and ointments are usually used, but not steroids because they can slow healing.

Steroids do have a place in treating other eye problems, particularly periodic opthalmia, or moon blindness, a recurrent inflammation of unknown cause. One theory is that it's an overreaction to the parasite onchocerca or another agent. In addition to showing signs of inflammation in the eye, the horse may be sensitive to light. As with other eye problems you should act quickly to prevent extensive damage. Local treatment with steroids and antibiotics can control a flare-up, especially if the drugs are started promptly, but usually another will follow. The disease can affect the retina and the iris as well as the cornea, which may become clouded and develop cataracts.

Small tumors on the eyelids and the nictating membranes are common and can nearly always be removed surgically. Other eye problems, such as glaucoma, are rare in horses. When cataracts appear independent of periodic opthalmia, they are usually congenital, and veterinarians haven't had a great deal of success in removing them.

It's important to remember, though, that such problems are truly uncommon. If your horse's eyes are damaged, it will probably be through injury or irritation. To prevent that, make sure his stall and paddock are free of sharp, protruding objects. (Some horses manage to cut their eyelids on their water buckets, where the handle curves under to hook into the bucket; you can cover the ends of the handle with tape.) And check the eyes as part of your daily grooming routine. Use water and a clean gauze pad to clean the area around them, and call the vet if you see any sign of unusual discharge or inflammation.

5. The Skin and Coat

Like all good packaging, your horse's outer wrapping is attractive—a glowing coat and flowing mane and tail help make him beautiful. But skin and coat aren't there just for looks: Both play important roles in keeping him healthy.

Skin forms a solid barrier that keeps out bacteria, viruses, and other invaders. If your horse gets an infection, the agent will enter through a gap in this armor—a cut, or an unprotected opening, such as the mouth or nostrils. The millions of nerve fibers that underlie the skin help prevent injury by alerting the horse through his sense of touch; they also allow you to control him and communicate with him through your hands and legs when you ride.

With the coat, skin also plays a role in regulating the horse's temperature. The coat is wonderful insulation for winter, growing long and shaggy as days grow short. In summer, sweat glands in the skin cool the horse through evaporation, while blood flowing through a network of capillaries just below the surface carries away heat from deeper tissues.

Keeping your horse's skin and coat in good working order requires nothing more or less than hard work: a vigorous daily grooming. When you groom the coat with brushes and a curry comb, you do more than get out dirt. You loosen and remove old, dead skin cells that can clog pores. You stimulate circulation at skin level, so that both skin and coat are better nourished. You also give yourself an opportunity to check the horse inch by inch, looking for small chunks in the skin armor and the first signs of skin trouble.

You'll find instructions for grooming in the section "Basic Care" and for treating wounds in the section "Troubleshooting," under "First Aid for Emergencies." Some other skin problems are discussed here.

SKIN PROBLEMS

If you spend hours grooming your horse, nothing is more up-setting than seeing his skin erupt in bumps or bald patches. Fortunately, most skin problems are easily treated; only a few spell serious trouble.

Saddle sores are spots rubbed raw by ill-fitting tack. A saddle of any style should be chosen to fit the horse just as much as the rider. It should clear the horse's withers amply or it will rub the area raw, and it should distribute weight evenly to the broad muscles that flank the spine without pressing on the spine itself. Saddles and bridles should be cleaned regularly and kept supple with oils and dressings, not only to preserve them but also to prevent chafing.

Saddle pads and fleece girth covers are designed to protect the horse's skin from rubbing leather. If the saddle fits well, the pad needn't be particularly thick, but it should always be clean to reduce the chances of skin diseases. Chlorine bleach will help kill germs as well as keep pads white. A pad that's made of a material that breathes well and absorbs sweat—quilted cotton, for example, rather than synthetic fleece—should go next to the skin on a horse that's prone to heat bumps. A second, thicker pad can always be placed over it if need be; special extra-thick foam pads are sometimes helpful for horses that have sore or especially sensitive backs.

Saddle sores usually clear up quickly if they're kept clean and dressed with a little antibiotic ointment—and if the tack problem is corrected. If your horse has a bad sore, you might stay off his back for a few days to give it a chance to heal. Saddle acne is raised, pus-filled bumps that pop up in response to pressure from tack, especially in hot weather. Hot compresses and astringents will help draw out the inflammation.

Ringworm is a common fungal infection that produces round, red, itchy, bald patches in the coat. The fungus takes root in the hair follicles, below the skin, and it can spread quickly through a barn, carried by brushes and blankets. Over-the-counter skin medicines often aren't effective: They may contain steroids, which can worsen the condition, or antibiotics that aren't specific for it. Sometimes, too, the condition is complicated by secondary infections. Your veterinarian may have to try several medications before the ringworm is wiped out. Meanwhile, to keep the problem from spreading, make sure each horse has his own set of brushes, blankets, and saddle pads. Disinfect them with chlorine bleach.

Onchocercias is another itchy, lumpy skin condition, this time appearing mostly on the belly. It's caused by the parasite onchocerca: The tiny worms migrate under the skin and die, setting up irritation. Steroids will help the itching, while de-wormers take care of the parasites.

Horses can break out in hives in an allergic response to many agents—feed, pollen, drugs, insect bites. Steroids and antihistamines can bring hives down, although usually they go away on their own in a day or two. If they reappear you should make an effort to find out what's causing them. Repeated exposure, especially to insect bites, can make some horses so sensitive and itchy that they rub themselves raw, a condition that has the common name "sweet itch." Steroids can help alleviate the itching, but getting rid of the cause is the best plan of action. Fly repellents and sprays can help here, since insect bites are the most common cause of the itch.

Hard lumps that look like small hives but stay around may be collagen granulomas—lumps of degenerated collagen tissue. Why these lumps develop isn't known, although allergy is suspected. If they interfere with the saddle they can be removed, or they may be resorbed under treatment with steroids.

Sarcoids are slow-growing, wartlike tumors. They're ugly but harmless, which is good, because they're difficult to get rid of. They have a tendency to grow back when surgically removed. New techniques tried with some success include radiation therapy and cryosurgery. Mast cell tumors are also noncancerous. They appear as lumps, usually around the head or at the knee or hock. Sometimes the hair falls out and the skin becomes inflamed. Unlike sarcoids, these tumors are usually easily removed.

Melanomas are tumors of pigment-producing cells, and they may or may not be cancerous. Most gray horses over fifteen—and many younger ones—have at least some of these tumors, most often at the base of the tail. Veterinarians usually adopt a wait-and-see approach because melanomas rarely cause trouble but often reappear and spread when they are removed. Sometimes, however, benign melanomas turn malignant and spread to internal organs, in which case there is little to be done. While cancer is rare in horses, older ones occasionally suffer from lymphosarcoma, a cancer of the lymphatic system. It appears as multiple soft lumps along the horse's sides. The horse usually shows other signs of illness, including depression and weight loss. There is no treatment, and the disease is fatal.

Any discussion of medical ills is likely to cast a pall of gloom, if not hypochondria; this chapter is probably no exception. But fatal, untreatable diseases like cancer truly are rare. Most of the time, if something's wrong with your horse, it will turn out to be something you can fix. And even more often, equine ailments are preventable. We'll turn now to some specific programs you can set up to guard your horse from these problems.

CHAPTER V

Preventive Maintenance

"Homeostasis" is a $100 word for balance, the balance your horse seeks to maintain with his environment. When he's resting in his stall, his lungs draw just enough oxygen and his heart pumps just enough blood to keep his body supplied, no more and no less. If he walks across the pasture, his muscles work just hard enough to produce the action required—there's no great effort and no wasted energy.

Put a rider on the horse's back and ask him to gallop across the field, and the picture changes. The demand to gallop sends flurries of messages racing between the brain and the body systems. Muscles spring into action and send out a stream of signals listing their demands—they must have more fuel and oxygen. And the horse responds. Arteries leading to the muscles open wide to give them what they need. As a result, blood pressure starts to fall, prompting the heart to pump harder and faster. As the demand for oxygen increases, the horse's breathing also becomes deeper and faster.

Every part of the horse must adapt to meet the challenge of the gallop or face damage and injury. If bones, muscles, and tendons aren't strong enough to take the pounding, they'll break or tear. If respiration and circulation can't supply enough oxygen, the muscles will work anaerobically, and toxic byproducts will start to build up. If these chemicals aren't cleaned out quickly by the circulation, they'll damage the fibers. Meanwhile, the work produces heat, which also must be disposed of. The horse begins to sweat, which depletes his supplies of fluids and essential body chemicals.

This is stress—a force that destroys the horse's natural resting balance and challenges him to restore it. Exercise stress is only one of the forces that can upset the horse's natural balance, though; the horse is beset by challenges from all quarters. You can help him meet them through the care you give him.

1. Conditioning

One of the biggest favors you can do your horse is to make him work. He might not see it that way, but—assuming that he's healthy and that you're not asking him to do things beyond his ability—work can be your first line of defense against the leading cause of breakdowns, exercise stress.

Just any old work won't do, though. You can't hop on the horse once a week, gallop hell-for-leather cross-country for a couple of hours, and expect anything but trouble. To give him the protection you want, your horse's work should be part of a carefully planned and closely monitored conditioning program.

You're now familiar with the ways that stress affects bone and muscle—making them stronger, to a point, or damaging them when the stress exceeds their limits. The same holds true for the respiratory-cardiovascular chain that supplies bone and muscle with the oxygen and nutrients they need. Conditioning work plays on this effect by applying measured amounts of stress, enough to wake up the mechanisms that will strengthen the horse but not enough to harm him. As the horse becomes gradually stronger, the stress levels are continually increased, so that he builds slowly to his full potential. A long cross-country ride that might have lamed him months earlier becomes a piece of cake.

DEVELOPING A CONDITIONING PROGRAM

There are so many variables in conditioning that each horse's program should be tailored individually. The program given later in this chapter is designed for an adult horse that's gone soft after several months of pasture rest. It should make him fit enough for serious performance work, such as hunter-jumper showing, low-level eventing, reining, cutting, and so on. The program takes about three months and can be adapted to suit most horses in similar circumstances. A horse that will be working only as a pleasure hack can get fit enough for that work in less time; one that will go on to more demanding sports, such as racing, endurance riding, or upper-level eventing, will need more time. In this case the work should be added at the end of the program and should be tailored to the kind of performance he's slated for—bursts of speed for the runner; long, slow rides for the endurance horse.

Other situations also demand more time. The older the horse and the longer he's been out of work, the longer it takes tendons and bones to adapt. If you're bringing a horse back from an injury such as a bowed tendon, you'll want to go extra slowly and monitor the horse very carefully so that you minimize the risk of a flare-up of the old problem. And a young horse that has never been conditioned will need six months or longer to reach a basic level of fitness. In these cases most of the extra time should be given to the early stages of the program, when the horse will be doing work that gradually develops bone, tendon, ligament, and hoof strength.

Whatever program you settle on, don't assume that the horse is fit just because you see well-defined, rippling muscles beneath his coat. Muscles build up much faster than bones, cartilage pads, ligaments, tendons, and hoofs, and if these underlying structures aren't strong, the horse will get in trouble as soon as he starts serious work. This is one of the most common conditioning errors, and many professionals are just as guilty of making it as amateurs. It's one of the reasons that knee chips, bowed tendons, bucked shins, and cracked sesamoids are so common on the track.

The catch is that it's very difficult to judge how strong most of these structures are—healthy hoof walls can be seen, but the rest of the hoof is hidden from view. Bones don't become wider with conditioning; they get denser, and the central cavities of long bones get narrower. These changes often can't be seen even on X rays. Ultrasound scans may reveal some changes in density, but for most people this technology is out of reach, geographically or financially. So in a sense, you're operating in the dark. The only course is to do the right type of work over a long enough period of time and trust that the adaptive changes you want are taking place. Meanwhile, you should be watching the horse carefully for even mild heat or soreness in the joints—signals that you're rushing your conditioning work and injuring the bones and joints.

Cardiovascular fitness is easier to judge, if you know what to look for. Here, too, there are elaborate technological aids —electronic heart-rate monitors that strap on with the saddle, giving you a continuous readout as you ride, and blood tests that, taken right after work, will reveal everything from levels of red blood cells and fluids to how well the horse is mobilizing supplies of free fatty acids and glycogen. These aids are helpful and may be worthwhile for a professional trainer, but they're expensive. You can probably learn enough through careful observation and close monitoring of the horse's vital signs.

The most useful of these signs is the heart rate, and to monitor it, you'll have to establish baseline values before you start your program. The two things you want to know are how much the horse's pulse increases with work and how quickly it recovers to a resting rate of 40 or 50 beats per minute after work stops. To get the baseline, give the horse five minutes at a medium trot and then hop off and take his pulse immediately—you have to act fast because the rate will start to drop at once. Two good places to find the pulse are under the jaw, where the mandibular artery runs along right next to the jaw bone, and at the back of the leg just above the fetlock, where major arteries run between the tendons. Count the pulse for ten seconds and multiply by six to get the working rate. Then walk him for fifteen minutes, checking the pulse every five minutes to see how quickly it drops and levels off. Next, give him a couple of minutes at a strong, forward canter and repeat the procedure—hop off, take the pulse, and check again at five-minute intervals.

Make a record of the baseline rates for comparison when you start your program. Recheck every week or so; as the horse gets more fit, his pulse will rise less—perhaps to 100 rather than 120 at the trot, and to 140 rather than 160 at the canter—and will recover faster. This will tell you that it's time to increase the length and speed of your workouts.

A post-work heart rate of 160 is a threshold for most horses —it signals that the heart hasn't kept pace with the muscles'

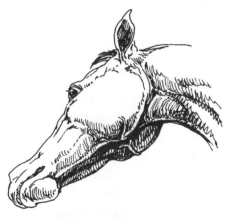

To check the pulse, find the mandibular artery—inside either branch of the lower jaw, at the notch in the edge of the jawbone.

demand for oxygen and that the muscles have switched over to anaerobic burning. For the first two months of a three-month program you'll want to stay below this rate. Think of your program as a series of building blocks: Slow work lays the foundation by strengthening the horse's heart and framework; speed work, added gradually, builds the fast-twitch muscles and puts on the finishing touches.

Respiration and temperature are less accurate monitors of fitness, but watching them can help you guard against over-stress, especially as work levels increase. Like pulse, respiration increases with work; as the horse becomes fitter it increases less and recovers faster. Generally a respiration rate that's higher than the pulse (a situation called inversion) is a danger signal—the horse has been pushed beyond his limit, and work should stop at once. Respiration can trick you, though. On hot, humid days the lungs will work harder just to help cool the horse, and he may pant, taking rapid, shallow breaths. Likewise, temperature shouldn't rise higher than 102.5 with work and should drop to normal within fifteen minutes or so; if it goes higher or stays high, the horse is seriously overheated. But again, weather plays a role: You can expect the horse to get hotter and cool out more slowly on a hot day.

Even with these monitors, it's easy to overdo your conditioning work. You're trying to walk the fine line between helpful and harmful stress, and if you err by slipping off to the harmful side, you want to know it before serious damage is done. One of the best ways to find out is to watch carefully for subtle changes in your horse's attitude. The horse under too much stress may start to seem lazy and unwilling when you ask him to work, or he may seem cranky and sour. Rather than becoming healthier and more alert, he may seem listless and start to drop weight. The signs of overwork vary from horse to horse, so it's important to know your horse's personality well.

A NINETY-DAY CONDITIONING PROGRAM

This program is presented as a sample work schedule that will bring a typical adult horse to a basic level of fitness. It shouldn't be blindly applied to any horse; adjust it to suit your horse's age, his starting level of fitness, and even his temperament (a "hot" horse tends to stay fitter when he's not working and get fitter faster than a lethargic one). Take into account such factors as terrain—a short canter uphill can equal the cardiovascular effect of a much longer one on flat ground—and weather. You'll be able to do less work on hot, humid days, and if you don't want to risk injury, frozen ground will limit you to walking.

The program is divided into ten-day segments, gradually increasing in level of difficulty. Don't go on to the next level until you see (from your horse's decreasing pulse and respiration, and other signs) that he can handle the current level well. Work five or six days a week, making the other days holidays for the horse. At the first sign of soreness, back off, rest the horse for a few days, and then (if he's sound) start work again at the preceding level.

Days one through ten: Walk, gradually increasing from twenty to thirty and then forty-five minutes. Keep the horse moving along briskly. Take him out of the ring to places where he'll encounter some easy hills, but avoid steep ones. Toward the end of the ten days, add a brief trot, just fifty strides or so on level ground, to each workout.

Days ten through twenty: Begin to replace some of the walking with trotting. Start with a three-minute interval; a day or two later, add another. Increase the two trot intervals to five minutes each by the end of the period. Don't press the horse to trot fast; let him pick the speed.

Days twenty through thirty: Gradually increase the total riding time to one hour by adding additional five-minute trots, walking between each trot. By the end of the period, you should be sandwiching six of these trot intervals into your workouts.

Days thirty through forty: Replace two of the five-minute trots with slow canters, each lasting three to five minutes.

Days forty through fifty: Add first one and then another canter interval, increasing your work time to fit them in. Begin to increase the speed, too, so that by the end of the period the horse is moving out at a medium canter.

Days fifty through sixty: Continue to gradually increase the speed of your canters, always watching carefully for signs that you're overtaxing your horse. By day sixty, your workouts should last an hour and fifteen minutes, divided between fifteen minutes of canter (in three-minute intervals), twenty to twenty-five minutes of trot (in five-minute intervals), and thirty-five to forty minutes of walking between the other gaits.

Days sixty through seventy: Gradually increase your riding time to an hour and a half, dividing the extra fifteen minutes mostly between the walk and trot. By this time, your horse should be ready to begin firing up his fast-twitch fibers; start by replacing one of his canter intervals with two minutes at a brisk hand gallop at a speed of about 450 meters a minute. (You can learn to estimate your speed if you mark off a 450-meter course and have a friend time you as you gallop it.)

A pleasure horse, who won't be asked for anything terribly demanding, can probably safely stop when he can do this much work without signs of stress; other horses should continue.

Days seventy through eighty: Replace a second canter interval with two minutes of hand galloping, and then a third. Remember to walk and trot between the gallops until the horse is fully recovered from them; use his breathing as a guide. And do this galloping work only two or three days a week— on other days, stick to walk, trot, and canter. Rather than increasing your riding time beyond the ninety mintues you're already doing (since every step is a jolt to the horse's legs), start doing some of your trot intervals up gradual hills.

Days eighty through ninety: As the horse's heart rate indicates that he's not over-stressed by the hand gallop (by staying below 160), increase your galloping speed to 500 meters a minute, a medium gallop. Again, gallop just two or three days a week, and always give the horse a chance to recover fully between the intervals.

A horse that can do this work comfortably is probably ready for whatever specialized training his sport calls for. Several days a week, replace the conditioning work with schooling in dressage, reining maneuvers, or whatever he needs to learn. Continue your conditioning rides on other days to keep him in shape. But remember to keep the program balanced so he's still doing the most physically stressful work on no more than half of his workdays. For example, barrel racing or jumping, which are stressful sports, can replace the work you'd do on galloping days. Basic dressage, which taxes the horse less physically, can replace a light workday.

A horse in a high-demand sport will need more conditioning before he's asked to compete. For endurance horses, you'll want to increase the total work time by adding more and more slow work to get his aerobic performance to its maximum; for a racehorse, you'll want to add more speed. The idea is that the horse should build slowly to whatever level of stress he'll face in competition. And whatever work is called for, only careful conditioning can give the horse the foundation to perform it.

2. Feeding for Health

You don't expect your horse to perform without food any more than you expect your car to go without gas, but how much food does he need, and what kind is best? In many barns, feeding is haphazard: Horses are given whatever feed is cheap or readily available at the time, rather than the one that's best suited to their needs, and it's measured out in coffee cans rather than weighed to get the proper amount for each horse. Good nutrition requires more thought than this. But the knowledge you need to give your horse a proper diet isn't especially difficult to master.

All horses need the same basic nutrients, but the amounts they need may vary according to the age and size of the individual horse, the amount of work he's doing, and other factors. The best available guidelines are those established by the National Academy of Sciences; follow-up studies at several clinics have shown that the amounts they set forth are ample for most horses. These are the guidelines used here. To apply them to your horse, you'll need to provide one piece of information yourself: his weight. If you don't have a livestock scale handy you can estimate his weight by measuring his girth with a weight tape, which is available at most feed stores.

THE BASICS: ENERGY, FIBER, PROTEIN

Energy is the first item the horse's diet must provide, and his need for energy increases along with his workload. Energy levels in feeds are usually measured in megacalories (Mcal). A horse who's doing no work—just loafing in the paddock— needs about 1.5 megacalories for every 100 pounds of his body weight. If he's on full-time turnout, he can easily get this from pasture grass. If not, hay is the best source. A pound of alfalfa or similar legume hay provides a tad over 1 megacalorie; a pound of grass hay, about nine-tenths of a megacalorie. So a typical horse that weighs between 1,000 and 1,100 pounds can maintain himself nicely on fifteen to eighteen pounds of good quality hay, as long as he's not working.

In work, the horse needs more energy than hay alone can provide. You can give it to him by replacing some of his hay ration with grain, an energy concentrate. How much grain to give depends, again, on how much work he's doing. A horse in light work—one who's just starting his conditioning program, for example—doesn't need much more energy than one who's resting. You can figure on about 1.7 megacalories for every 100 pounds of weight. Oats provide 1.5 megacalories per pound, so our typical horse should do well on thirteen to fifteen pounds of hay and about four pounds of oats. Corn provides 1.75 megacalories per pound, and barley 1.63; you'd feed correspondingly smaller amounts of these feeds. Commercial mixed feeds, such as sweet feed and pellets, usually have slightly fewer megacalories than oats, about 1.4 per pound.

A horse doing medium work—an hour or so of trotting and cantering, with perhaps a few jumps—needs about 2 megacalories for every 100 pounds of weight. Ten to twelve pounds of hay and about seven pounds of grain would be right for the typical horse. When he starts doing harder work, with a lot of galloping, his energy needs will go as high as 2.5 megacalories per 100 pounds of weight. You can up his grain ration to ten pounds or more.

There's a limit to how much grain you can add to your horse's diet, though, and that limit is set by the horse's digestive tract. Horses need a certain amount of fiber; without it, heavy loads of carbohydrates in the digestive tract can prompt laminitis, tying up, and colic. Grain alone doesn't provide enough (it's only 10 to 12 percent fiber, compared to 30 percent or more for hay). A good, safe rule of thumb is to make sure that fibrous foods, like hay, make up about 50 percent of the diet. But since hay fills up the horse without providing enough energy for high performance sports like racing, trainers in these sports are in a bind. One solution is to switch the horse's grain ration to corn, the most concentrated energy source.

Energy is only part of the story. To maintain and replace his body cells, the horse has a continual need for protein. Protein needs are highest while the horse is growing, and once he reaches the age of two they drop off. An adult horse's diet should contain at least 8.5 percent crude protein, regardless of how much work he's doing; 10 percent should cover most horses' needs amply. Depending on the feed, a lot of the protein is lost in digestion, so he'll probably actually get the benefit of two-thirds of this amount. But more isn't better; the horse can't store the amino acids that are the building blocks of protein and then recall them on demand. Instead, they just form fat.

Most pasture grasses range from 9 to 18 percent crude protein. Alfalfa hay has 16 percent. Barley is the most protein-rich grain, at nearly 14 percent, followed by oats, at 13.6 percent. Corn has considerably less protein, about 10 percent. It would seem difficult for a horse's diet to be deficient in protein, but it can happen. For example, timothy and some other grass hays are just 9 percent protein or less; if the hay is late-cut and stemmy, it will be harder for the horse to digest and he'll get less protein out of it. If a horse is getting only grass hay, and corn for his grain ration, he may not get enough protein. The best way to avoid this situation is to mix and match high- and low-protein feeds. Make part of the grain ration oats or another high-protein grain, or make part of the hay ration alfalfa or another legume hay.

VITAMINS AND MINERALS

You may be tempted to add some insurance to your nutritional program by slipping a vitamin-mineral supplement to your horse's feed each day, and there are plenty on the market to choose from. But be careful. In most cases supplements aren't necessary, and even when they're needed they should be chosen carefully because imbalances and excesses of certain vitamins and minerals can poison your horse.

Most of the vitamins a horse needs are either synthesized in his intestines or are amply available in good-quality grain and forage. To start at the top of the alphabet, vitamin A helps the horse's skin and mucous membranes stay healthy. He can get all he needs and more from green grass and fresh hay, especially legume hay. Since this vitamin deteriorates rapidly, though, hay that's been stored over the winter may have lost most of its vitamin A content, a situation that may call for a supplement.

The daily requirement for an adult horse is 11.36 IU for each pound of body weight, or 11,360 IU for a 1,000-pound horse. Most supplements provide more because, like the vitamin A in hay, the vitamin A they contain deteriorates as the product sits on the shelf. It probably won't hurt your horse to get a bit more than the daily requirement, but since his body stores extra vitamin A, the excess can build up and perhaps become toxic. That means you'll want to stop the supplement when he again has access to pasture or good quality hay.

Of the B vitamins, horses are known to need thiamin, riboflavin, and pantothenic acid. (Other B vitamins may be helpful too; the need just hasn't been established.) All are amply present in grains and forages. Grass hays and corn, though, have less thiamin than other feeds, and a horse who gets only these feeds may be low in this vitamin—just as he may also be low in protein. The solution is to supplement or to add other feeds, such as oats, that are richer in thiamin. The B vitamins are less likely to be toxic than vitamin A because they are water soluble; what the horse doesn't need, he just eliminates.

Whether or not horses need vitamin C isn't known. Vitamin D, on the other hand, plays an essential role in maintaining the skeleton and regulating calcium levels. With too little vitamin D, the skeleton loses calcium and the joints swell and become stiff. With too much, calcium is deposited in the tendons, ligaments, and blood vessels as well as the bones.

Normally there's no need for a vitamin D supplement; it's synthesized from sunshine and sun-cured hay, and the only horses who are in danger of developing deficiencies are those that can't get either. A supplement may be called for if the horse is shut in all winter and fed poor quality hay; 3 IU per pound of body weight (or 3,000 IU for a 1,000-pound horse) is thought to be enough. Levels have to build to fifty times the normal requirement before toxic signs are seen, but since this vitamin is stored in the horse's body, toxicity can occur. Jessamine, a wild pasture plant common in the South and Southwest, contains a chemical that mimics vitamin D and produces the excessive calcification typical of an overdose.

Requirements for vitamin E and vitamin K haven't been established, but both are thought to be needed by the horse—vitamin E for muscle management, vitamin K for blood clotting. A typical diet seems to give the horse several times the amount of vitamin E he needs. Vitamin K is thought to be synthesized by the helpful microorganisms in his intestines.

The two minerals that probably cause the most confusion in horse feeding are calcium and phosphorus. The horse must get enough of both in his feed, and he must get them in the right proportion. Both minerals circulate in the horse's system and are used in basic body functions and maintenance; when blood levels fall low the body simply takes what it needs from the skeleton. If that goes on for a while the bones will start to become weak and porous. But blindly supplementing with these minerals is dangerous: If the horse gets too much phosphorus, it will block the absorption of calcium; if he gets too much calcium his bones will become overmineralized and brittle.

The ideal ratio is two parts calcium to one part phosphorus, although the ratio can be three to one or one to one without causing trouble. Grass (and grass hay) is perfectly balanced and contains plenty of these minerals for an adult horse. The problem comes when grain is added—grains, especially corn, are much higher in phosphorus. These are two ways out of the problem. One is to feed a commercial grain mix that's labeled "balanced"; it won't disturb the good ratio of your grass hay. The other is to balance your grain by adding a supplement or by switching over to alfalfa or another legume hay, since these hays have more calcium than the grass hays. Remember to add grass hay back into the diet if you cut back the grain ration, though, or you may end up with too much calcium.

A horse that's given free access to a salt block will balance his own intake of sodium, and if you make sure he has a mineralized block he'll take care of his needs for a number of other trace minerals at the same time. There is a long list of such minerals, believed to be necessary in tiny amounts for various body functions. Most (including potassium) are present in good quality feed and forage, and a horse who is on a good diet and has a mineralized salt block generally won't develop a deficiency. Supplementing can be dangerous, since some minerals, such as iodine and selenium, can be toxic in relatively small concentrations. However, in some areas certain minerals are deficient in the soil and thus lacking in the grass and hay that grow there. A veterinarian can tell you if such deficiencies are common in your area and what supplement, if any, you should add to your horse's feed.

WATER AND ELECTROLYTES

If your horse has free access to fresh water, he'll regulate his own intake, as he should. The only time you should regulate it for him is immediately after hard work. At that time his circulation is concentrated in his muscles and near his skin; his intestines are under supplied. He may be very thirsty, but a big drink might send his digestive tract into cramps and set off a case of colic. Offer water a few sips at a time until he stops breathing hard and his temperature drops to normal.

At other times he should have all the water he wants, whenever he wants it. There's no set amount—work, hot weather, an intestinal illness, or an increase in the amount of food he eats can all increase his need for water anywhere from 20 to 300 percent. You just have to keep checking the bucket, or install an automatic waterer in his stall. (If you use an automatic waterer, make sure the horse knows how to use it before you leave him for a day with it.) You can tell if a horse is dehydrated by pinching a fold of his skin. It should snap right back; if it stays folded up for a moment, his fluid levels may be dangerously low.

Electrolytes are electrically charged versions of essential minerals that affect many body functions including the regulation of fluid levels. The major ones are sodium, chloride, potassium, calcium, and bicarbonate. Under normal circumstances the horse will get all the sodium and chloride he needs from a salt block (sodium chloride is table salt) and the others from his feed. But in really strenuous work, such as eventing and endurance riding, quantities of electrolytes are lost through sweat. The problem is compounded in hot weather, and illness can also cause the horse to lose electrolytes. When electrolytes are low, the horse won't retain enough fluids and he'll rapidly dehydrate. Low levels of calcium, potassium, and bicarbonate contribute to muscle cramps, tying up, and thumps.

This is why trainers in high-stress sports often offer their horses electrolytes that are available in solution or in powders to be mixed with water. If you think your horse may need them, you should ask your veterinarian what solution to use. Electrolytes should always be given with a bucket of pure water alongside, so the horse won't be forced to take in more of these minerals than he needs just to satisfy his thirst, and they should never be mixed with feed at some predetermined dose. Too much is harmful—high levels of sodium will make the horse retain too much water, and high levels of calcium and potassium can affect his heart.

SETTING UP A FEEDING PROGRAM

The tables in this chapter, adapted from those devised by the National Academy of Sciences, show sample diet proportions for horses at various ages and levels of work and the amounts of nutrients contained in certain feeds. To set up a feeding program for your horse, figure his needs according to his weight and workload and then select feeds that will meet them. (If you want to use a commercial mixed feed and you're in doubt about its nutrient content, the manufacturer should be able to provide information.) You may find that you have to adjust levels and types of feed as you go along. Some horses, particularly those that are nervous or high-strung, burn up energy faster than others, and if the horse has been ill or under-nourished you may have to build him up. Watch for signs of deficiency: Weight loss indicates too little energy in the feed; loss of appetite is a classic sign of a diet too low in protein (although it can also signal that the horse is ill).

TABLE 1: Sample diet concentrations satisfying basic requirements for horses at various ages and levels of work*

SITUATION	DIGESTIBLE ENERGY (MCAL/ POUND OF FEED)	GRAIN (%)	ROUGH-AGE (%)†	CRUDE PROTEIN (%)	CALCIUM (%)	PHOS-PHORUS (%)	VITAMIN A (IU/LB FEED)
Mature horse, maintenance	1.0	0	100	8.5	0.30	0.20	725
Light work (pleasure, etc.)	1.1	25	75	8.5	0.30	0.20	725
Medium work (jumping, cutting)	1.3	50	50	8.5	0.30	0.20	725
Hard work (racing, polo)	1.4	65	35	8.5	0.30	0.20	725
Yearling (12 months)	1.3	45	55	13.5	0.55	0.40	900
Two-year-old (light training)	1.3	30	70	10.0	0.45	0.35	900

* Adapted from "Nutrient Requirements of Horses," 1978, by permission of the National Academy Press, Washington, D.C.
† Hay containing 1 Mcal/lb.

But be wary of giving too much of a good thing. Vitamins and minerals aren't the only components of the diet that can cause harm in excess. A diet that's too rich in energy and protein is expensive, will make the horse fat, and may prompt colic or founder. Some recent research even suggests that over-rich diets are to blame for a lot of the bone problems experienced by growing horses, by prompting too rapid growth. Your goal should be to give the horse what he needs, no more and no less.

Because the horse's digestive system is designed to process food in small amounts, split your horse's ration into at least two and as many as four meals a day. Make sure the diet contains enough fiber to keep the intestines working smoothly —don't worry that your horse will develop a hay belly from it; a hay belly is the result of too little exercise rather than too much hay. If your horse has heaves or a similar respiratory problem that's aggravated by dust, look into beet pulp and similar dust-free high-fiber feeds.

Consistency is important. Feed the horse at the same times every day (his digestive system doesn't like surprises) and, after a big meal, wait an hour before hard exercise, to give the intestines a chance to at least get started on digestion before you call his blood supply out to his muscles. There is no reason why a horse can't be fed after work, provided three criteria are met: The work in question is the usual amount at the usual time, the horse is completely cooled out and recovered from. it, and the meal is the usual amount at the usual time. When you make a change in the horse's feed, do it gradually. Start by mixing a small amount of the new feed into his usual ration, and slowly increase the proportion over a period of days.

Shopping for feed can be confusing, but since quality makes a difference it's worth the effort. Hay should smell fresh and be absolutely dry; reject it if the bales are damp or show any sign of mold. Early-cut hay is leafier and less stemmy than late-

TABLE 2: Nutrient contents of common feeds*

FEED	DIGESTIBLE ENERGY (MCAL/LB)	CRUDE PROTEIN (%)	CRUDE FIBER (%)	CALCIUM (%)	PHOS-PHORUS (%)
Alfalfa hay,					
early	1.09	17.2	31	1.75	0.26
late	0.98	15.0	34	1.29	0.24
Barley (grain)	1.61	13.9	6	0.05	0.37
Bermudagrass,					
grazed	0.99	9.1	28	0.49	0.27
Blugrass, grazed	1.11	17.0	26	0.56	0.40
Corn (grain)	1.75	10.9	2	0.05	0.30
Fescue, meadow,					
grazed	1.04	11.5	29	0.60	0.43
hay	0.92	10.5	33	0.57	0.37
Oats (grain)	1.52	13.6	12	0.07	0.37
Sorghum (grain)	1.60	12.6	3	0.03	0.33
Timothy hay,					
early	1.00	11.5	31	0.50	0.25
late	0.90	9.0	32	0.41	0.19

* Adapted from "Nutrient Requirements of Horses," 1978, by permission of the National Academy Press, Washington, D.C.

cut hay, and therefore has a higher nutrient value (which means you'll probably pay more for it). But good quality hay cut in any season should be relatively free of weeds and stubble. Store hay in a dry place, and stack the bales so that air can circulate among them to prevent dampness and mold from building up.

Grains also vary in quality, depending on the amount of fiber and chaff they contain. A bushel of top-quality grain will weigh more than a bushel of lower-grade and will provide more digestible energy. This is why you should feed by weight, not measure—if you feed by the scoop and the quality of your grain varies from one delivery to the next, you could inadvertently change the amount of food your horse is getting. Grains should also smell sweet and be mold-free. Be particularly wary of moldy corn, which is often hard to spot, since some of the molds that grow on corn can be highly toxic to horses. Make sure that corn and other grains are stored dry.

If you choose a commercial mix, go with a name brand from a reputable dealer. This gives you some assurance that the contents won't vary radically from batch to batch and that the feed will be fresh. Commercial mixes have advantages and disadvantages. Sweet feeds are blends of grain mixed with molasses; the sweetener makes them tasty, but it also makes them spoil more rapidly than straight grain—three weeks is about the longest you'll want to keep them around. Pellets keep longer, and some contain high amounts of fiber (a help when good hay isn't available). But horses generally find them less appetizing.

If you want to keep your horse on pasture, you'll need about two acres of good-quality grass per horse; even then, you may have to supplement with hay and, if the horse is working, grain. Improving the pasture by fertilizing and seeding can increase its yield; the nearest Cooperative Extension Service office is a good source for information on what types of high-nutrition grasses do well in your area. It's also worthwhile to divide your pasture in two, so that one side can recover while your horse grazes the other. If you have only a small area, pick up manure once a week. This controls parasites and also increases your pasture yield, because horses usually refuse to graze in areas where droppings lie.

TABLE 3: Vitamin contents of common feeds (mg/lb)

FEED	CAROTENE (A)	RIBOFLAVIN	THIAMIN	E
Alfalfa hay	11.8	4.8	1.4	40.8
Barley, grain	0.5	0.8	2.3	8.2
Corn, grain	1.1	0.7	1.0	11.7
Oats, grain	0.05	0.8	3.3	8.4
Timothy hay	4.1	5.6	0.8	28.6

3. Basic Care

Along with good conditioning and feeding programs, basic daily care provides the best insurance you can get against a breakdown. This chapter is concerned with the details of horse ownership—stall mucking, foot cleaning, grooming, deworming, and so on—that some people revel in and others find pure drudgery. But whether you view them with joy or distaste (and whether you do them yourself or hire someone to do them for you), they're worth close attention. These details not only prevent trouble, but following up on them gives you a chance to spot problems when they first begin to develop.

In most areas of horse care, there are many methods and many schools of thought, each with passionate advocates. Rather than advocating one or the other, this chapter will stick to general guidelines and point out how they relate to the health of the horse.

STABLE AND PASTURE

Many people believe that if horses could be turned out twenty-four hours a day, a lot of the health problems they have would never get a chance to develop. This is a logical view—nature never intended the horse to spend most of his life cooped up in a barn, get meals only at set times, and get all his exercise in one brief and stressful hour. Respiratory disease, thrush, arthritis, and the whole line of stable vices have been blamed on the practice of keeping horses in barns. Yet for lack of pasture space, climate, or simple convenience, most horses simply can't be kept turned out. And since even the best stable is an unnatural environment for the horse, it should be designed carefully to minimize potential problems.

The exact type of stable that's best depends a lot on climate. In the Southwest, heat is a major problem; in the Northeast, severe winters. But all stables should be well ventilated. This means leaving the tops of the walls between stalls and aisle and between the stalls themselves open, with grillwork between if the horses tend to get after each other. Windows and doors should be designed for good cross-ventilation; if the roof has a sizable overhang, they can be left open even in rainy weather. Cupolas or roof vents are essential, especially if hay is stored in the barn's loft, and in hot areas fans should be used to keep air moving through. Although your barn should be well ventilated, in cold-winter climates you also have to be concerned about drafts, which can chill the horse much more than a drop in temperature. It goes without saying that barn walls should be solid, without gaps and chinks; windows and doors should be designed to close snugly when winter winds whip up.

Stall frames and walls should be sturdy—along the lines of 2-by-6-inch oak planks. A kicking horse can easily shatter a lesser board and get seriously cut up in the process. Ceilings should be high, and doorways should be both high and wide. All surfaces should be free of loose nails and sharp projections; door latches, for example, should lie as flush as possible to the door. A horse that shies in the aisle can get a nasty puncture wound from a projecting bit of hardware. For similar reasons, the aisle should be free of tack trunks and like paraphernalia, and any window the horse might possibly reach should be protected by wire mesh. Store hay and especially grain in a place where the horse can't possibly get at it, or you may have a case of founder or colic on your hands.

If you have a choice, a 12-foot-square loose box makes better quarters for an adult horse than does a straight stall. A horse can lie down in a straight stall, but he can't turn around and stretch out the way he can in a box. There's also greater danger of the horse getting cast (wedged against the wall so that he can't get up in a straight stall, although some horses just seem to have a natural talent for this in any stall. If yours is one, bank the bedding against the walls and try putting him in an anticast roller, which fits around the girth and may prevent his rolling in the stall. Most horsemen agree that it's

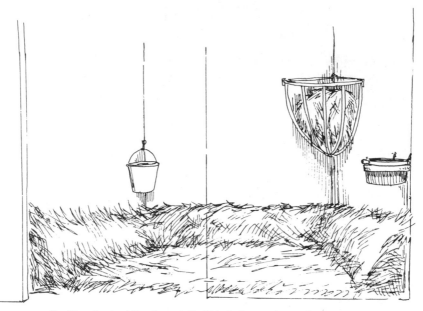
Banking the bedding in a stall will help keep a horse from getting cast.

safer to leave a horse without a halter in a loose box; there's always the danger that the horse will slip a foot in the halter or get it caught on something and be injured. If the stall has a hay rack (or if you use a hay net, which hangs on the wall) make sure it's high so the horse can't get a foot caught in it— horses have a habit of pawing at their food. If it's low enough to be a danger, remove it and give the hay on the floor.

Grooved or textured concrete makes an ideal aisle floor— it wears well, can be scrubbed down or hosed, and is non-slippery. Good stall floors have been made of asphalt, clay, packed earth, heavy lumber, and rubber matting, and have been bedded with straw, shavings, peanut hulls, shredded newspaper, and other materials. Each material has advantages and disadvantages. Asphalt lacks resilience but lasts forever; lumber is softer but eventually will rot; shredded newspaper (available by the bale) is expensive but dust-free and thus ideal for horses with respiratory problems. More important than the material, though, is the way it's kept: If you want your horse to keep his feet, the stall should be clean and dry at all times. Wet and soiled bedding should be removed and replaced daily. With a dirt or clay floor, which holds moisture, you may have to clean more often and more thoroughly than you would with a paved floor; on a paved floor, add extra bedding to cushion the hardness.

Periodically, the stall should be stripped and the floor disinfected. Chlorine bleach mixed with water makes an excellent disinfectant for this job, as well as for disinfecting aisles and other barn surfaces. An occasional scrubbing all over the barn will do a lot to check disease. You should also be wary of letting dust and cobwebs build up in corners and on rafters; a heavy load of dust will complicate any respiratory problems. Clean out feed and water buckets regularly, too; the slime that can build up in them is unsanitary as well as unappetizing.

By this time, you're too aware of the importance of exercise to leave your horse standing in the barn for days on end. But even if you're giving him daily exercise under saddle (or on a longe line), he needs free time outdoors. Whatever stabling setup you have should permit access to a paddock, if not a pasture, where the horse can roll, buck, or just stand in the sun for at least a short time every day. This will help his health and his mental outlook, too. Possibly the ideal setup is a stall with a door that opens directly into a paddock, so the horse can virtually come and go as he pleases. An arrangement like this will also cut down on stall-cleaning chores, since the horse will be outside much of the day.

Pay as much attention to the safety of a pasture as you would to the safety of a barn. Barbed wire and cattle guards are fine for cows, who are phlegmatic enough to steer clear of them, but are disastrous for horses, who may run right up against these barriers or try and fail to jump them. Also avoid flimsy fences and wire fencing with gaps large enough to entangle a hoof. Rubber fencing material was popular at one time but caused problems because horses would chew it, injest bits of rubber, and colic. Probably the best fencing material is still solid, heavy lumber. Electric fencing is fine; the current isn't enough to injure a horse, and most horses develop a healthy respect for it after one brush. So that the horse won't charge into the single wire of an electric fence and snap it, though, this type of fencing should be strung along a wooden fence that will provide a visual barrier.

A horse that's turned out full-time needs some sort of shelter from the elements, such as a run-in shed. It should open away from the prevailing winds. And turnout shouldn't mean that the horse is out of mind as well as out of the barn— make sure he has plenty of water, whatever supplementary feed he needs, and the same daily care as a stabled horse. It's safest to turn a horse out without a halter, for the same reasons that it's safest to leave the halter off in his stall. However, if your horse is the hard-to-catch type, you can use a special safety halter that will come apart if it gets caught on something. Or you can improvise one by adding a breakaway strap—a thin strap that will tear easily—to the headpiece of his regular halter.

GROOMING

Obviously you don't need to polish your horse as if you were headed for a show every time you take him out for a hack, but daily grooming is as important to his health as it is to his appearance. Good care will keep his skin and coat in top condition, so that when you do show, he'll have the glow and polish that only health can bring. No feed supplement or coat polish can replace elbow grease; if you want your horse to shine you'll have to work at it.

You'll want to clean your horse up before you ride, so he'll be presentable, but after work is a better time for a deep, thorough grooming. Work (through the sweat it produces) loosens the dirt, grease, and dead skin cells that lie on top of the skin, so they're easier to remove. This scurf not only dulls the coat and provides a breeding ground for germs, but also interferes with the evaporation of sweat, the horse's natural cooling method.

To get it out, start with a curry comb, working in circular motions over all the fleshy areas of the body. Apart from loosening scurf and dead hair, the curry comb should give a good massage to the skin and the muscles beneath it. Use a flexible rubber curry comb so you can bear down on it to get the full benefits of the massage; a metal comb will be too harsh. You'll have to stop every so often and knock accumulated dirt out of the comb. Avoid sensitive areas, such as the face. Here and throughout your grooming, be on the lookout for cuts and sores; daily grooming provides you with a ready-made opportunity for troubleshooting.

Next take a dandy brush, which has thick, stiff bristles, and brush all over the horse in the direction of the hair growth. Use brisk, firm strokes—your goal is to remove the coarse dirt and hair you loosened with the curry comb—but ease up a bit around the head and in other sensitive areas. Work the brush right down to the roots of the mane and the dock, since dirt often builds up in these areas. But don't brush the long tail hairs briskly (in fact, some people don't brush them at all but simply separate them by hand) because they break and pull out easily.

When you've done the whole horse with the dandy brush, go back and brush again with a body brush, which has finer, shorter bristles. This brush will remove the fine dust and dirt from the coat. Every few strokes, scrape the brush clean by drawing it across your curry comb. If you want the coat to shine like a satin mirror, go over it a final time with a rub rag, still working in the direction of the hair, to take off the last traces of dust.

If the areas around the horse's eyes are dirty, clean them with a fresh cotton ball or gauze pad dampened with warm water. Use cotton or a dampened sponge to clean around the mouth, nose, ears, and tail, too. Watch all these areas carefully for signs of infection or unusual discharge, so you'll be able to treat developing problems early.

Now turn your attention to the feet. Clean out each one in turn. Use your weight against the horse's side or shoulder to get him to shift his weight to the opposite leg, and then ask for the foot you want by running your hand down the back of his leg and squeezing gently at the fetlock. Horses have a natural reflex that prompts them to lift a foot when something bothers the fetlock, and after you've done this a few times the horse will learn what you want and may even have the next foot waiting for you before you ask for it. Use a hoof pick to remove dirt and foreign objects from the sole, working from heel to toe so that you don't accidentally jab the sensitive frog. A stiff-bristled brush will remove finer dirt. Again, be on the lookout for trouble—thrush, corns, bruises, cracks—so you can take the appropriate action.

As long as the feet are in good condition, though, they probably won't need any other daily care. Hoof dressings are supposed to keep the hoof moist, but many veterinarians say they do more for the owner than the horse—you think you're helping, but you're really not. The hoof's moisture is supplied by the circulation from within; while some hoof dressings may help a very dry foot, most just sit on the surface and are wiped off as soon as the horse walks through grass or bedding. Hoof polishes, which dry like nail polish, can do harm because they interfere with the hoof's natural moisture balance—a good hoof is designed to lose some moisture through the outside walls. To compound the problem (and really mess up the hoof), some people sand the hoof wall to get a smooth surface for the polish, removing the outer layer of horn that should regulate the moisture balance. Applying thrush medication as a preventive is another bad idea, since these preparations are extremely drying. Wait until you see signs of the problem before you start treatment.

On a daily basis, basic grooming is all you need to do. But from time to time other grooming measures will help keep your horse happy and healthy. In warm weather, when the horse sweats a lot during work, he'll appreciate being sponged off with clear water afterward. And there are times (especially if your horse is a gray or has a lot of white markings) that you'll want to give him a bath. Use a large sponge and a bucket of warm water mixed with the minimum amount of a mild livestock shampoo—strong detergents (and too-frequent baths, for that matter) can dry the skin and dull the coat. Some horses don't mind being rinsed with water from a hose; others will be happier if you use a warm-water rinse and a bucket and sponge. At any rate, never aim a hose at the horse's head. You'll upset him, and water could get in his ears or nostrils. Finish the bath by removing excess water from the coat with a body scraper, working with the hair, and walk him dry. If the air has a hint of a chill, put a cooler on him while he dries; in cold weather, skip the bath altogether and just spot-wash any stained places to avoid chilling the horse.

Cold weather creates a different grooming problem: clipping. A horse that's not in work won't need to be clipped, but one that's doing any work at all probably will. When the heavy winter coat gets soaked with sweat, it can take forever to dry. As long as it's wet it has no insulating value to speak of, so the horse can get thoroughly chilled. A clipped coat will dry faster, but remember that the horse will need a stable blanket when he's not working, to replace the layer of insulation you're removing.

Many people clip the horse all over, but field hunters and other horses that work outside in cold weather are often clipped only on their bodies, with long hair left on their legs and perhaps under the saddle. Another option is a trace clip, in which only the areas that sweat most heavily—the throat, chest, and belly—are trimmed. Wait until the winter coat is fully grown in before you clip, unless you want to do it again later in the season. Getting an even clip is a skill that takes a bit of practice, and if you've never used electric clippers it's a good idea to get someone to show you how. Some horses object strenuously to the whining clippers, so make your first attempt with a quiet one—it won't make things easier to have the horse jumping around as you try to work.

If you have a stallion or a gelding, you should clean his sheath every three months or so, or however often you find

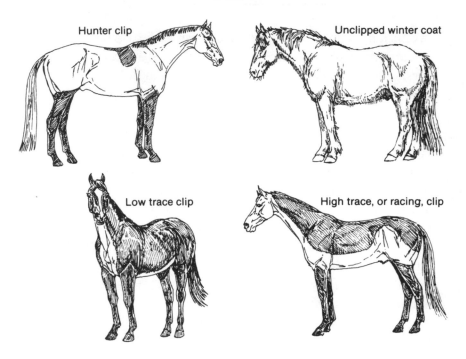

Hunter clip

Unclipped winter coat

Low trace clip

High trace, or racing, clip

he needs it. Dirt and discharge can build up in the sheath, making the horse uncomfortable and eventually leading to an infection. Horses are sensitive in this area, so you may want to enlist a helper and use some form of restraint, such as a twitch or putting the chain end of the lead line over the horse's nose. Be careful to stand at the horse's side, facing back, and don't lean down so low that you'll catch a hoof if he kicks up. Use warm water and mild soap to sponge gently up inside the sheath; then rinse with the sponge and clear water. Most horses will accept this if you work slowly (some will even let you flush the area with a hose); if yours objects strenuously, your vet can tranquilize him to do the job. A mare's udder should also be sponged off periodically.

Less often—every year or so—you should have your horse's teeth checked. Uneven wear can leave hooks and ridges that may irritate his cheeks and his tongue, prevent him from chewing his food properly, and make him uncomfortable in his bit (flipping the head and other signs of discomfort in the bridle often signal tooth problems). If this has happened, the teeth can be floated, or filed, by a veterinarian.

TRIMMING AND SHOEING

In the wild, a horse doesn't need shoes—he simply doesn't subject his feet to the pounding that can break up the horn. His feet don't need trimming, either, because his near-continual movement wears the hoof wall down in pace with new growth. All that changes when people decree when, where, and how the horse will exercise. Metal shoes are nearly always needed to protect the feet, and because the shoes prevent the hoof wall from being worn down naturally, the feet have to be trimmed.

Good trimming and shoeing, done in the right way at the right time, make an enormous difference in keeping the horse sound. Most adult horses need shoeing roughly every five to eight weeks, but this is so variable that you're best off if you watch your own horse carefully and set up a schedule to get the blacksmith to your barn before the shoes get loose or the feet outgrow them. Loose shoes are dangerous, not only because they can be lost: A loose nail can work into the sensitive tissues of the foot or push out, cracking off a piece of the wall. When you clean your horse's feet, check the shoes—try to move them on the foot. If they shift at all, the horse should be reshod. Other signs to look for are heels that have grown out over the sides of the shoes, shoes that are worn or have slipped back or sideways on the feet, protruding clinches or gaping nail holes, and a tinkling noise when your horse walks on pavement. These signs show that the horse is overdue for shoeing, so take note of how long it's been since the blacksmith's last visit and try to get him there sooner next time.

Farriers talk a lot about shoeing a horse level and in balance, which confuses many people. In a horse with ideal conformation, it means that both sides of the hoof wall will be the same height, so that when the hoof is viewed from the front, a line bisecting it will be perpendicular to the ground. Both front feet will match, and both hind feet will match. However, few horses have ideal conformation. If one leg is just slightly crooked, the hoof will meet the ground at an angle. In nature, the walls would wear unevenly so that eventually one would be slightly higher than the other. If you trim the hoof walls so that both are the same height, however, you force the hoof to land unnaturally—first one wall, then the other—and throw the bones in the leg out of alignment. It won't be long before soundness problems develop. A good farrier will watch the horse move and trim his feet so that both sides of the wall touch down together, even if the result is a less than perfect-looking foot.

Another angle that's best left to nature is the slope of the hoof when viewed from the side. This should nearly always match the pastern angle, even if it appears to be too steep or too shallow, because inside, the bones of the foot and the pastern line up. Trimming to add more slope to a steep hoof (or less to a very angled one) compresses the bones and asks for trouble.

As for the shoes themselves, there are dozens of types for

HOOF TRIMMING

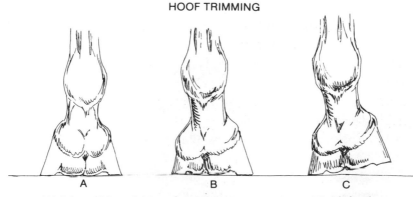

(A) A foot with straight conformation, correctly trimmed, lands level. (B) When crooked foot is trimmed naturally, both sides meet the ground at once. (C) If the crooked foot is trimmed artificially "level," one side lands before the other.

special purposes, but unless you have an unusual need—such as a soundness problem, which we'll take up in the next section—simplest is probably best. A basic fullered shoe (with a central groove ringing the arc) is standard for most riding horses. Toe grabs, heel caulks, and ridges of borium (a hard metal) are used to add traction in special circumstances, but for general riding they're best left off—that bit of extra traction can give the foot and leg an unexpected wrench.

Shoes that are hot-forged to fit the foot are best, but even when ready-mades are used, the shoe should always be fitted to the trimmed foot, rather than the foot trimmed to fit the shoe. One rule of thumb that some farriers use is that the shoe should extend beyond the wall just enough to roll a dime all the way around. This gives the wall room to expand. Inside, the shoe should rest completely on the wall and never put pressure on the sole.

DEWORMING

Until recently, deworming was either traumatic (the vet inserted a long tube through the horse's nostril and down his esophagus to his stomach, and pumped medication in) or largely ineffective (oral medication was mixed with feed, and the horse refused to eat it or sprinkled half of it on the stall floor). But new products, methods, and theories have changed that. While it's probably impossible to keep a horse parasite-free, there's no reason why the population can't be kept below harmful levels with an antiparasite program that deals with both the horse and the environment.

The parasites that affect the horse are inside him for only part of their life cycles; they also spend some time on the ground. Usually parasite eggs are passed out of the horse in manure. They hatch, and another horse ingests larvae as he grazes. A few enter by different means—botflies lay eggs on the horse's coat, and he injests them from there (they look like tiny yellow seeds, and you should scrape off any you find).

Habronema larvae are carried to open wounds by stable flies and live within the wound, creating what is known as a summer sore. In any case, the chief goal of an antiparasite program is to reduce the population of parasites in the horse's surroundings, so he won't pick up so many.

Pasture management and sanitation are highly effective in reducing parasite populations. Resting a pasture for two months or more breaks the life cycle of many parasites—there simply aren't horses around to pick up the larvae. Keeping stalls clean and picking up manure from paddocks (and pastures too, if possible) on at least a weekly basis removes parasite eggs before they can hatch. One thing not to do is to spread stall manure on your pasture as fertilizer—you could be scattering worm eggs along with it.

Even with good management, chances are that you'll need to use chemical deworming medications regularly. These preparations work by killing adult and maturing parasites in the horse, before they can lay eggs. There are a lot of preparations on the market, but no single one is effective against all parasites, and in a few cases parasites have developed resistance to certain medications. A relatively new medication, ivermectin, is popular because it kills most major parasites (including immature stronglyes, which are among the most dangerous to the horse) and seems fairly safe. But even this medication isn't perfect; it won't kill tapeworms, a pest that about two out of five horses carry. That means that you should use a variety of medications in your deworming program, in rotation.

There are two schools of thought on deworming schedules. The traditional view holds that, since many parasites mature in about two months, deworming should be done about that often. The schedule should be varied to fit individual requirements, though. If you're keeping your horse in a crowded stable, he'll likely be picking up more parasites and may need medication as often as once a month; if he has twenty well-managed acres to roam, he may get by with less frequent dewormings. If you're in doubt about the effectiveness of your program, ask your vet to do a series of fecal egg counts on manure from your barn.

Some research suggests that a deworming program can be just as effective if it's concentrated in the time of year that parasites are most active. In the northern states, this is late spring and summer; three wormings spaced over this time may be enough to keep the population down for the whole year. If you want to set up a program like this, consult your veterinarian to find out when parasites are most active in your area. Whether you choose a seasonal or year-round method, take a "herd health" approach—all the horses in the barn should be treated at the same time, or the ones you treat will be immediately reinfected by the others.

Tube-worming is still probably the best way to ensure that the horse gets a precisely measured dose of medication (it's not painful for him, just upsetting), and some horses will gobble up deworming medications in their feed. However, oral paste wormers have become popular for several reasons. You can learn to administer them yourself without too much difficulty (it's too risky to try the tubing yourself; if you slide the tube down the trachea by mistake, you could kill the horse). The pastes come in premeasured doses, loaded into syringes for administration, and you can be relatively sure that the horse gets the full dose if you take a few precautions.

Before you administer the paste, rinse the horse's mouth out and make sure he's not carrying a wad of hay or grass in it—otherwise the paste will stick to the food, and he may be able to spit it out. Put the syringe in the side of the horse's mouth and deliver the paste toward the back of the tongue (but not down the throat). He should swallow it all. When you choose a paste, make sure the dose in the syringe is right for your horse's weight. If you dose a 1,200-pound horse as though he weighed 1,000 pounds, your worming program will be less effective. And since most of the medications are toxic at some level, you don't want to exceed the recommended dose.

VACCINATIONS

Like deworming programs, vaccination schedules should be custom tailored to fit your circumstances. The vaccines most commonly given protect the horse from flu; rhinopneumonitis; eastern, western, and Venezuelan equine enchephalomyelitis; and tetanus. Less commonly, horse owners also vaccinate against strangles, botulism, and rabies. Most vaccines work in the same way: They trick the horse's immune system into thinking the disease is present so he produces antibodies; should the real germs enter, the waiting antibodies will knock them out. But to be effective, each vaccination has to be given at the right time.

The shots for flu and rhino confer immunity for only about three months. For a horse that's stabled alone or with a few others, a shot once or twice a year may suffice; his risk of exposure to these diseases is low. If your horse travels to shows or meets, or if he's at a boarding stable where other horses come and go, his risk of exposure is much higher. You should give these shots in three- or four-month intervals.

The encephalomyelitis shots last about six months, but in cold-winter climates it's not necessary to provide year-round immunity. The diseases are carried by mosquitoes, so an annual shot given in early spring, just before these insects emerge, should cover the horse until frost kills them off in the fall. In warm-winter climates, you should renew the shot in the fall. Vaccines are available against all three varieties, singly or in combination; which ones you give depends on where you live or expect your horse to travel. The Venezuelan strain has so far been reported only in the South and Southwest, for example, so if you live in New England you probably don't need to worry about it. Check with your veterinarian to see which strains he recommends vaccinating against.

Tetanus toxoid is essential—the tetanus bacteria are literally everywhere in most barns—and should be renewed annually (keep your own immunity up to date while you're at it). Shots for strangles, botulism, and rabies are given annually in special circumstances. Both strangles and botulism seem to affect some farms and barns more than others; those that have had problems often vaccinate. Until recently strangles vaccines haven't been invariably effective, but a new vaccine, developed at Cornell University, is due on the market and promises better immunity. Vaccinating against rabies may be advisable if you have had a high incidence of the disease among wildlife in your area.

Like deworming medications, vaccines are best given to all the horses in the barn at once to help check the spread of disease. However, sick horses shouldn't be vaccinated, and those that are undernourished or carrying a heavy burden of parasites often respond poorly. Don't stress the horse on the day of vaccination. Rarely, a horse has a mild reaction to a vaccine, losing his appetite or running a low fever. This shouldn't last more than a day and can usually be prevented the next time by using a different type of vaccine.

HEALTH EXAMS AND RECORDS

As vigilant as you are in watching your horse for signs of disease and other problems, you can still miss them. Some things just take a trained eye to spot. So it's a good idea to have your vet check the horse periodically. This needn't cost a great deal, especially if you combine the checkup with worming or immunization so that you don't pay for an extra barn call. When to do it depends, again, on your circumstances. An annual checkup is fine for a horse that leads a quiet life. One that has a busy show schedule might be checked three times—before, during, and after the show season. Growing horses or pregnant mares should be checked much more frequently, of course.

Keeping accurate records of health care will also help you

prevent problems. Anytime the vet or blacksmith visits, mark down the date of the visit and what was done—shoes reset or replaced, horse tube-wormed, or whatever. Make your record detailed. If the horse gets a vaccination or medication, for example, mark down the name, manufacturer, amount, and method of administration. This will help you remember what treatments worked and whether your horse has bad reactions to certain medications. Note any signs of trouble in your records, too—the horse didn't finish his evening grain, for example, or seemed slightly off in work—and the amount and type of work the horse does each day. Should a problem develop, you'll be able to give the veterinarian an accurate history.

Your records should also include the baseline values for the horse's vital signs—his respiration rate, pulse, and temperature—taken at rest, while the horse is in his stall. There are standard normal ranges for each of these signs: respiration, eight to sixteen breaths per minute; heart rate (for an adult horse), 28 to 40 beats per minute; temperature, 99.5 to 101.5. But the resting figures vary from horse to horse, and it's sometimes difficult to tell if a problem is developing when you don't know what's normal for your horse.

Because any activity (or even the anticipation of activity) can raise the values, disturb the horse as little as possible when you take your readings. Count respiration from outside the stall by watching the flank rise and fall for ten seconds and then multiplying by six to get the breaths per minute. Take the pulse under the jaw, at the mandibular artery, again counting for ten seconds and multiplying by six. Take the temperature with an equine rectal thermometer, attaching a string to the loop on the end of the thermometer and then clipping the string to the tail, so that it won't fall out and be stepped on.

Take several readings at different times and on different days and average them; then add your figures to the horse's permanent record. They'll help you and your vet determine whether slight changes are significant.

MAINTENANCE SCHEDULE

The schedule given here is for an adult horse. Where a range is given, the interval should be set according to individual circumstances (climate, workload, and so on).

	Daily	Weekly	Monthly	2 Months	3 Months	6 Months	Annually
Exercise and/or turnout	x						
Basic grooming	x						
Clean feet	x						
Shoeing				x———x			
Clean sheath					x		
Check teeth							x
Worming (year-round method)				x————————x			
Vaccinations:							
influenza					x————————————x		x
rhinopneumonitis					x————————————x		x
E/W/VEE						x————x	x
tetanus							x
Health exam							x
Clean stall	x						
Strip stall, disinfect		x					
Barn cleanup (remove dust, disinfect)			x				
Paddock/pasture cleanup		x					

4. Coping with Stress

Exercise stress causes more breakdowns than any other type, but it's not an isolated factor. If you want to keep your horse sound and healthy to a ripe old age, you have to keep the total stress picture in view. For example, it may seem ridiculous to suppose that horses are exposed to emotional strains. But in fact, they are—anytime they're placed in a situation that runs counter to their instinctive patterns of behavior. And when people enter the picture, that happens often.

Horses developed as herd animals who roamed free over the plains. But in pasture herds, emotional stress can be high. In any group of horses, a natural pecking order develops, and the low horse on the totem pole may be alternately shunned and harassed by his pasturemates. In the wild this doesn't usually create problems—the herd is fairly constant, so each horse knows his or her place, and there's plenty of room to get out of the way if the harassment gets out of hand. But people turn horses out in confined spaces, and often the makeup of the group changes every day. Each horse must establish his rank again and again, and the low-level ones won't be able to avoid what's bound to be an unpleasant situation.

When you take a horse out of that situation and stable him for twenty-three out of twenty-four hours in a day, the stress levels are even higher. Confinement itself is unnatural. And things are even worse if he's stabled alone, without the company of other horses, because horses are social by nature. Add to that a host of unfamiliar sights and sounds—tractor engines, wheelbarrows—and confusing new demands from trainers, and you have a stress level that, from the horse's point of view, would equal that of any Wall Street job.

The horse's initial reaction to emotional stress is to put his systems on alert. Chemicals secreted by the brain, epinephrine and norepinephrine, are responsible: They prompt the pulse and respiration to increase, open the arteries leading to the muscles, and raise blood sugar levels. The horse's muscles tense, anticipating the need for action. He becomes animated, even jumpy; the slightest sound may send him shooting forward. In the barn, he may move restlessly about his stall. But most of the time this reaction doesn't continue for long. To varying degrees, horses are remarkably adaptable. Over time they become acclimated not only to confining pastures and barns but to situations that are far more unnatural—riding in vans and trailers, for a common instance, and directing city traffic or performing next to predatory animals in the circus for more exotic ones. What once was frightening becomes routine.

Some horses do not adapt as readily as others, though, and continued levels of emotional stress have clear effects. Horses under stress commonly develop stable vices. They weave back and forth in their stalls or kick the walls repeatedly; crib, chewing any wood surface they can lay their teeth on; or wind-suck, gulping air as they chew. These vices can be damaging—a horse can go lame kicking his walls or wear his teeth down chewing wood, so that he can't grind his food.

But even without such direct damage, a horse who's under emotional strain will suffer physically. With his body going on alert all the time, he needs more food, so he's apt to be a poor keeper (a horse that requires a larger than average ration to stay in good condition). That puts the owner in a quandary because giving him extra food will also boost his energy levels, with the result that he'll be even more nervous and animated. A better solution is to find the factor in the horse's environment that's causing the stress. He may simply need to get out more. He may be feuding with the horse in the next stall. If he's alone, he may need company (some people keep a goat as a companion for a nervous horse).

Even if your horse is well adapted to his surroundings, an abrupt change can trigger stress reactions. You can sidestep most of them if you stick to consistent routines—feeding and exercising at the same time each day, for example—and introduce new demands gradually. If you want him to trailer quietly to his first show, start a few weeks beforehand by

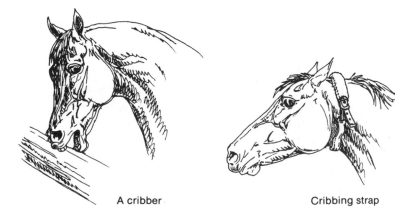

A cribber   Cribbing strap

loading and unloading him a few times. Then graduate to slow rides around the block; by the time show day comes, he'll be an old hand.

An exercise program can also reduce psychological stress: It promotes a general sense of well-being; as the horse becomes more capable, he's less apt to be fazed by your demands; and frequent workouts get him out of the barn and reduce boredom. If you do a fair share of your work cross-country, you'll be exposing him to new surroundings, and he'll gradually become desensitized to the cows, cars, and other monstrous objects that may terrify him at first.

EXPOSURE

Nature gave the horse a normal body temperature of 99.5 to 101.5 degrees, and, like all warmblooded creatures, he must maintain it no matter what outside conditions prevail. When winter temperatures drop below freezing and the wind whips by at forty miles an hour, he has to find a way to keep warm. When the summer sun sends the mercury up into the nineties, burning the pasture brown, he's got to cool down. Extremes in temperature and climate are stress: They challenge the horse to maintain his natural balance.

The horse has two basic methods that he uses together to meet this challenge: He can regulate the amount of heat that leaves his skin and the amount that is produced in his muscles. Both methods are triggered by special centers in the brain that are alert not only to changes in the outside temperature but to minute fluctuations in blood temperature. And his body goes through some seasonal changes that help him to put the methods into action.

As days grow shorter, he begins to lay in a layer of subcutaneous fat and to grow a long, wooly coat; both will act as insulators against the coming winter cold. Later, when temperatures drop, small branches of the blood vessels closest to the skin shut down, so that less blood flows near the cold surface and more heat is retained. In cold weather the horse will be more active, so his muscles generate more heat, and when temperatures are bitter he'll shiver—an all-over muscular activity that is even more efficient at producing heat than regular muscle contraction.

When the horse turns up his thermostat this way, he needs more fuel—just as you use more fuel if you turn up the thermostat in your house. Some estimates put the amount of extra calories he needs at ten percent for every ten degrees that the mercury falls below freezing. If he doesn't get the energy he needs from food, he'll take it from the stores in his body, first from the insulating fat layer and then from muscle and other essential tissues.

Apart from adequate food, the horse has another essential need in winter: shelter. Wind and dampness are his greatest enemies in cold weather—cold air rushing past the skin increases the heat loss from it, and a wet coat loses its insulating abilities. When a horse's temperature-controlling mechanisms fail him, first the outer tissues and then the vital organs grow colder; if things go far enough, he'll lose consciousness and die. But if he has enough to eat and can stay dry and out of the wind, even in a run-in shed in the pasture, he can probably weather the worst of winters.

In summer, the needs—and the mechanisms—reverse. The horse sheds his winter coat and his fat, and the small blood vessels near the skin open up again so that more blood will be carried to the surface to be cooled. On hot days, he'll seek shade and restrict his activity, so his muscles don't produce much heat. When his body temperature starts to rise above acceptable limits, he'll also bring a number of other mechanisms into play. He may take rapid, shallow breaths—panting—to keep a steady supply of cool air moving through his lungs, where it will help cool his circulating blood. He'll start to sweat, and the evaporation of the water on his skin will cool it. This mechanism works best in dry weather, when evaporation is quickest, so he'll feel the heat more on humid days.

Rather than extra food, his need now is for extra water and extra amounts of electrolytes, the trace minerals that are lost with perspiration. Summer sweat is different from winter sweat. The horse drinks more water in summer and his body fluids become thinner; he's able to sweat more freely, and because the sweat is thinner than winter sweat it evaporates faster. What's lost, though, must be replaced. The body gives cooling top priority over other functions and will continue to do so to its own detriment. If the total fluid loss reaches eight percent of the horse's body weight (about nine gallons), his life will be in danger.

If the cooling mechanism fails, the horse can suffer heat exhaustion. Sweating stops or diminishes, and the horse trembles and wobbles when he tries to walk. His temperature will shoot up and his breathing will be rapid and shallow. He may collapse.

Some horses are better endowed to cope with certain climates than others, and the key factor is the amount of surface area they present in relation to their body mass. The heavy breeds of horses and ponies that developed in northern Europe have thick layers of muscles and fat—every surface is rounded and bulging. They're better at retaining heat than losing it. Lean, flat-muscled thoroughbreds and Arabs, on the other hand, have less mass lurking under the skin. They cool off faster than the heavy breeds, but they also have a harder time keeping warm in the winter.

It's rare for a horse of any breed to die of exposure to heat or cold, of course. But much of what people ask horses to do plays havoc with the temperature-control mechanisms. A horse who does hard work in summer is in double danger of overheating—exercise, because it forces the muscles to work, also produces heat. Similarly, a horse who works in winter will make double withdrawals from his energy banks and may face another problem: To facilitate cooling out after work or for show-ring appearance, his shaggy winter coat will probably be clipped, and he'll lose some insulation.

This isn't to say that horses shouldn't work in anything less than ideal weather, just that some precautions are in order. A horse that has been clipped should be blanketed and stabled in cold weather. A horse that works in summer should be offered an electrolyte solution along with his water, and work should be cut back on hot days or when the temperature-humidity index rises over the 150 mark.

DISEASE

Infection triggers a complex set of responses in the horse, among them, localized inflammation, with the characteristic heat, redness, swelling (from an increased flow of blood and other fluids) and soreness; fever, which is as poorly understood in horses as it is in humans; and the immune responses mediated by the white cells of the blood. A respiratory infection produces increased mucus secretions. These responses play a role in fighting off the agents that have invaded, but at the same time they can be hard on the horse. Inflamed intestines don't digest food well, and he gets shortchanged on nutrients. Congested lungs supply less oxygen. It's even possible for the immune reaction to get out of hand and harm the horse, producing something like an allergic reaction. For example, it's thought that oversensitive lymphocytes may be responsible for some cases of the emphysema-like ailment, heaves.

Disease alters the horse's ability to deal with other kinds of stress because it forces his systems to operate at low levels of efficiency. And the knife cuts both ways—stress of any kind lessens the ability to fight disease. The mechanism through which it does this isn't fully understood, but one possible explanation is that among the body chemicals released in response to stress are steroids. In many animals (and some research indicates horses may be among them), steroids suppress the immune response. Thus a horse who is under emotional strain or is fighting the elements is a pushover for any passing bacteria or viruses.

In fact, the horse has only a given capacity for response to stress of all kinds. It may be great or small, depending on his overall health and condition, and repeated exposure to gradually increasing amounts of stress can increase it. Horses can learn to stand quietly while cannons are fired; they can get used to working in extreme climates; their immune systems gear up after exposure to a disease, so they can fight it better next time; and their strength and stamina increase with exercise. But putting a horse under any one kind of stress reduces his ability to cope with other types.

Since the type of stress you have most control over is exercise, this principle will obviously affect the work you do with your horse. You probably wouldn't think of starting an arduous training program while your horse was suffering from the flu, but it would be just as mistaken to start in the middle of a heat wave or on the day you move him to a new barn. Give his systems a chance to regain their balance before you add new weights to the stress side of the scale.

MINIMIZING STRESS

If you're going to ride your horse, show him, or do just about anything with him—and presumably, you bought him for some such reason—you won't be able to avoid stressing him to some degree. Indeed, you wouldn't want to avoid stress entirely; pretty soon he'd be a flabby and feeble excuse for his species. What you can and should do, though, is to minimize the harmful effects of stress, to get the maximum conditioning effect from everything you do with the horse while taking the least risk possible. And there are many steps you can take before, during, and after work to accomplish this goal.

For one, getting the horse dressed for work may involve more than putting on a saddle and bridle. If your horse has any tendency to interfere in his gaits, or if his work calls for great agility (jumping, or cutting and reining maneuvers, for example), boots may be in order. There are dozens of styles for various purposes: rubber bell boots that fit over the front hoofs to protect them from the hind hoofs; overreach boots that protect the back of the fetlock from the same danger; ankle boots that cover the fetlocks, and galloping boots that fit over the cannons as well, to protect them from blows from the opposite feet; and so on. Some people prefer leg wraps in place of boots.

Which style of boot you use depends on the horse's way of going and the kind of work he does. Many horses, for example, interfere behind or in front—they knock one ankle with the

  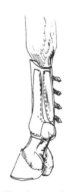 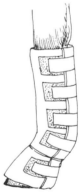

Galloping boot   Shin, or splint, boot   Tendon-and-ankle boot   Shipping boot

Ankle boot   Skid boot   Bell boot

opposing foot as they go. If your horse does this, you'll certainly want to use ankle boots whenever he works and when he's turned out, too. Jumpers often wear bell boots or overreach boots because there's a high danger of the front feet and legs being clipped from behind on landing. Reining horses often wear run-down boots, which protect their fetlocks from being scratched by the ground in sliding stops. Many trainers put boots of one kind or another on green horses because their inexperience often makes them a bit uncoordinated.

If you use boots, make sure they fit. If they're too loose, they'll slide down or twist around, chafing the skin and leaving the area they're supposed to protect unguarded. If they are too tight, they'll interfere with circulation or the working of the joint they're protecting. When the boot is put on correctly, you should be able to move it slightly on the leg but not shift it out of position. If your horse's ankles tend to stock up, or get puffy, when he stands in his stall, check the boots after you've been riding for twenty minutes or so. This type of swelling usually goes down when the horse begins to work and the circulation in his legs and feet improves, and if it does the boots could start sliding around.

Circulation is central to another before-work step: warming up. You have your horse tacked up and ready for work, but if you want to minimize stress you won't go out and start galloping right off the bat. Especially if he's been standing in his stall, his muscles are getting a minimum amount of blood—most of it is probably around his digestive tract, dealing with what's left of his breakfast. So start work slowly to give the arteries that feed the muscles a chance to open up and increase deliveries. For most horses doing basic work, fifteen minutes or so of brisk, forward walking and easy trotting will give the body systems a chance to prepare for exercise before they're asked to do anything demanding, and the horse will be less apt to strain muscles. But different horses may require longer or shorter warmups; begin work when your horse is relaxed, alert, and moving forward freely.

During work, whether you're training the horse or trying to improve your own riding, it's all too easy to get so caught up in what you're doing that you lose sight of how much stress you're loading on the horse. You're doing an exercise and you want to get it right, so you just keep repeating it long after you should have stopped. Try to be alert to signs that you may be asking too much from your horse. Watch his breathing—when he begins to huff, it's time to rest. Attitude is another yardstick—if he began the session willingly but is now getting cranky, you may have pressed too far.

Certain kinds of work are by nature more strenuous than others. Some of these are obvious. Jumping, for example, puts tremendous stress on feet and legs. The old adage "there are only so many jumps in a horse" probably contains more than a grain of truth, and many trainers feel that once a horse is trained, he shouldn't be jumped more often than once a week. If training requires him to be jumped more often than that, the fences should be as low and as few as possible.

Other kinds of work are high-stress but not so obviously so. Trotting and cantering small circles, for example, can be very hard on muscles, tendons, and ligaments, even though the movement appears simple. Work on a circle is basic in most training programs because it helps make the horse supple and responsive to your controls, but you should be careful not to overdo it. Remember that work on a longe line can be equally stressful; the horse may not be carrying a rider, but he's still going in small circles.

If you need more practice in riding than you can get on your horse without overworking him, one solution is to do some of your work on another horse. If it's the horse's training that's in question, though, you may have a problem. You won't want to finish the session with the horse being outright disobedient, even if his unwillingness stems from fatigue. When this type of situation comes up, the best thing to do is probably to go back to some simple maneuver that you know the horse does well, and end the day's work there.

During competitions, try to pace the horse. At shows, for example, use breaks between classes to rest him, taking off the saddle if you can and perhaps letting him graze in the shade. If you want him to last through a full day of classes, the breaks aren't the time for intensive, all-out schooling sessions; if his skills need touching up before he goes in the ring, keep the work to a minimum. For longer competitions, such as endurance rides and events, keep careful tabs on the horse's attitude and respiration, and slow down when he starts to tire. You may lose a bit of time. But if you don't listen to what the horse is telling you, you may not finish the ride at all.

Remember to adjust your work program for outside factors. If the horse was just wormed or vaccinated, give him a holiday; if he was just shod, go easy for a day or so until you're sure his feet have adjusted to the trimming. Cut back your work on hot days and be extra alert when you watch the horse's respiration for signs of fatigue. Take ground conditions into account, too. Both hard ground and deep, soft, or muddy ground can do harm—the hard surfaces because of concussion and the soft ones because the horse can slip or wrench muscles when his feet sink in. Avoid uneven surfaces, where it will be hard for the horse to put his feet down level. If you're caught on a stony trail, walk.

The basic idea behind all these precautions is to avoid doubling up stress by adding one type—exercise—to another, be it heat, illness, or whatever. You can apply the same rule to other situations as they come up.

Cooling out after work is even more important than warming up. A horse that's not cooled out properly is in danger from colic, laminitis, and muscle damage. When a horse finishes hard work, his heart rate, respiration, and temperature are all above normal. He's sweating, and his blood vessels are dilated and his circulation concentrated in his muscles and skin. If you put him back in his stall, blood can pool in his lower legs, causing muscle cramping higher up and perhaps contributing to laminitis in his feet. If you give him his fill of water or food, he might colic—the intestines are poorly supplied with blood at this point and unprepared for digestion.

The first rule of cooling out is to keep moving. This will prevent the blood from pooling because it will keep the heart rate slightly elevated and force the muscles to keep working, both of which will keep the circulation moving. As blood continues to circulate through the muscles, it will help bring their temperature down. So as soon as you finish your work session, get off and start walking with the horse; don't even pause to untack for the first few minutes.

As you walk, take the horse's pulse, at the mandibular artery, and check his respiration. Because you've kept a record of these rates throughout your conditioning work, you'll know whether the horse has been unusually stressed by the work you've done. Work can elevate the heart rate to 150 or even 200 beats a minute, but it starts to drop as soon as the horse slows down and should be back around 100 within a matter of minutes.

The manner as well as the rate of breathing will tell you a lot. A horse that breathes deeply is trying to replace the oxygen he used in exercise; one that draws rapid, shallow breaths is

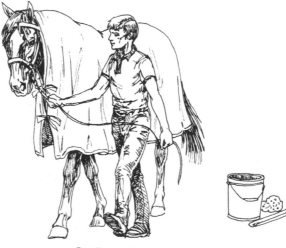

Cooling out

panting to help cool off. He may breathe so quickly that the respiration rate tops the pulse rate at first, and if this continues for more than five minutes or so it probably means that he's dangerously overheated. A sign of even more serious trouble is thumps, in which the horse breathes rapidly with visible muscle contractions in his flanks and a distinctive thumping noise. This is a sign of exhaustion; you should have a vet check the horse.

When you've walked for a few minutes, pause to untack. This is a good time to check the temperature, if possible. Even short workouts can raise the horse's temperature two or three degrees; harder work can raise it to 105 degrees or more. Like the pulse and respiration rates, though, the temperature should begin to drop rapidly. If the horse is in good shape and wasn't severely stressed, all these measures should be back within normal ranges in fifteen minutes or so. So continue walking, checking the rates after that time and then, if they're not down, rechecking every fifteen minutes.

In warm weather or when the horse is quite hot, you can help the cooling process by sponging or misting him with water; like sweat, the water will draw heat off the skin as it evaporates. Use your own judgment in this; basically, the hotter the day and the horse, the more water you can use, and the colder it can be. In extreme cases you could even sponge all over with ice water. But in cool weather, you'd run less risk of chilling the horse if you used tepid water and sponged only over the major blood vessels at the head, neck, chest, and inside the front legs. In cold weather it's also a good idea to throw a cooler over the horse as you walk: If the skin cools too rapidly, the small blood vessels near it may close down, and you'll lose the radiator effect of circulation.

Water on the skin is fine, but hold off on drinking water until you see that the rates have started to drop. Then let the horse drink a few sips at a time, walking in between. He's probably thirsty and would be glad to drink his fill, but until he's cooled out, doing so might send his intestines into cramps.

If he's worked hard or has sweated heavily, offer an electrolyte solution alongside the water.

When the rates are back to normal or nearly so—which may take anywhere from fifteen minutes to an hour—you can put the horse back in his stall. Leave him some water, but don't fill the bucket yet. And you can give him hay to help his digestive tract get started up again, but hold off on grain. The reason is that even though the rectal temperature is normal, the muscles can still be hot. After he stands for a few minutes, he may break out in a sweat again; you'll have to take him out and walk some more. So you should check back in fifteen minutes or so to make sure that all's well, and if he's done hard work wait an hour or so before you give grain. After hard work, it's also good to check back four to six hours later. This is when you'll see signs of colic or founder developing, and you should also be able to spot any hot or puffy areas in the legs, which may be signs of injury.

Some horsemen give the legs extra care after every workout, either rubbing them down with a brace or doing them up in wraps, or both. The value of these treatments is debated, though. A brace, such as liniment mixed with water, or even an alcohol rub, has a superficial effect. If the inner structures of the leg have been damaged by work, it won't do anything for them. If there is any benefit, it probably comes more from the massage involved in applying the brace than from the preparation itself. But a leg brace may feel good to the horse after hard work (although too much of this sort of thing can make the skin dry and scurfy). Use a mild preparation or a weak solution and rub gently but firmly up and down the lower leg for five minutes or so, or until the brace evaporates.

The theory behind wraps is that they'll help support tendons and prevent the ankles from swelling while the horse stands in his stall, as well as guarding them from injury. They probably will, but whether you want this on a daily basis is questionable. Some think that keeping the legs in wraps causes the tendons to lose tone: Since they have less work to do, they grow weaker.

And keeping swelling down with wraps doesn't alter whatever underlying problem is causing the puffiness—it just removes the external signs, so you lose one important way to measure the health of your horse's legs.

If you decide to wrap, be absolutely sure that your bandages won't interfere with the circulation to the foot. Use a quilted cotton pad or a similar wrap under the bandage, and make sure it lies on the leg smoothly, without wrinkles or folds. Then wrap with the bandage. The usual method is to start at or above the ankle and wrap down over the pastern and then back up to a point just below the knee. Finish by wrapping down until you run out of bandage (which will probably be about midpoint on the cannon). Each turn should overlap the one before by about a third of the bandage width. Keep the tension even and check it with each turn by inserting a finger under the wrap at the back of the leg, at the tendon. The bandage should be snug, but not so tight that you can't get your finger in. If you use a brace or liniment before you bandage, make sure it's mild—wrapping increases the heating effect of these preparations.

If you ship your horse to a show or some other event, you need to take extra precautions. Shipping involves a lot of stress. The horse has to be on his toes throughout the trip to keep his balance and stay with the movement of the trailer or van; he arrives at a strange place, surrounded by unfamiliar things. If your trip is a long one, it's a good idea not to work the horse hard on the day he travels. Most large shows will let you ship in a day or so ahead of time, so the horse can have some time to recover from the journey. You should also withhold grain on the day you ship—the last thing you want is a case of colic on the road—although the horse can have all the hay he wants.

Before the horse steps into the van or trailer, he should be fitted out with leg wraps or shipping boots—he could easily injure himself if he loses his balance as the trailer takes a turn.

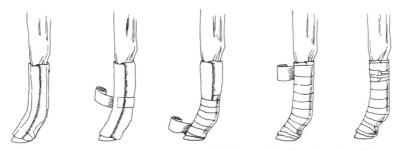

Put a pad around the leg, making sure it lies smoothly. Starting above the ankle, wrap down over the pastern, up to the knee, and back down until you finish.

Some horses are scramblers: When they feel their weight shifted by the motion, they panic and start to scramble around, and they may even fall. The best way to solve this problem is to give the horse extra room to spread his hind legs, so he can keep his balance better. If he's traveling alone, remove the center partition in the trailer or move the back end of it all the way over to the side. If he must travel with another horse, you can get the lower section of the partition cut out, so that the horses will be separated but your scrambler will still be able to spread his legs.

Cutting out the center partition gives a scrambler more room to spread his legs for balance.

If your horse is at all inclined to jerk his head up or rear when he's upset, a shipping helmet is a good idea. Many people also wrap the dock, to keep it from being rubbed by the back of the trailer, and use special fleece-padded shipping halters. The horse should be tied with enough slack to allow him to move his head and munch hay from a hanging net. But don't leave more than two feet or so of slack, or he may get a foot tangled in the lead. Many trailers are equipped with tie chains that are the right length. They should be fitted with breakaway snaps (or the lead should be tied with a quick-release slip knot) so you can get the horse out fast if you have to.

At the show, the best thing you can do to minimize stress for your horse is to stick as closely as possible to your usual routine. Give him the same feed he gets at home, at the same times; any sudden change in feeding can upset his digestion. Try to work him and groom him at the usual times, if you can, and give him some chance to relax, either grazing at the end of a lead or in a paddock, if possible. If he's stabled, make sure his stall is well bedded and safe. All these precautions will help ensure that the stress of traveling won't diminish his show performance or harm his health.

CHAPTER VI

Keeping Problems Small

In all probability, your horse will get sick or lame at some point in his life—the risks are just too many and the chances too high for him to avoid such problems entirely, even if you give him flawless care. His chances of recovery will be better the earlier you detect the problem, identify it, and start fighting back. A little extra vigilance on your part, for example, can make the difference between a mild lameness that keeps him out of work for a few days and a serious one that lays him up for weeks or months, or even leaves him permanently handicapped.

To spot problems, you first have to be thoroughly familiar with what's normal for your horse. Know his normal resting rates for temperature, pulse, and respiration. Memorize the contours of his legs, so that you'll be able to distinguish new bumps and swellings from old ones that have been there for years without causing trouble. Be familiar with his usual appetite (whether he's a greedy or a picky eater), and his general attitude (whether he's sluggish or rambunctious). Then, every time you visit the barn, be on the lookout for change of any kind.

1. Troubleshooting

Any shift from normal can signal trouble, but to take effective action you need to know what kind of trouble it is and how serious. And to know those things, you'll have to be familiar with the signs of equine illness, or at least the signs of the major and most common ones. Many of these signs were covered in earlier chapters; here are twenty-five that you should know, in checklist form for quick reference.

• Heat, pain, swelling, and redness are the classic signs of inflammation. As such, they can crop up anywhere—around an infected wound, an inflamed eye, and an injured joint. They're clear indicators of local trouble, and the degree to which they're present will help you determine how serious the trouble is.

• Loss of appetite and a depressed attitude signal illness, but they don't necessarily help identify the problem. A horse that won't eat may have colic, but some other problem may be causing him to turn up his nose at his food. If he mopes around his stall, he may just be tired, or he may be getting sick (if he hangs his head, he's probably seriously ill). You and your veterinarian need to investigate further.

A sick horse often shows a depressed attitude.

• A higher than normal temperature in a resting horse usually indicates infection, probably from bacteria or viruses. Again, you'll have to investigate—fever alone doesn't tell you what agent is at work or whether the infection is local or systemic. A high fever indicates a serious problem, but the fact that a fever is low doesn't necessarily mean that a problem is mild.

• A temperature reading that's significantly below normal (under 99 degrees, for example) can mean serious trouble—shock, severe chilling, or poisoning.

• Low weight and a poor, dull coat are usually signs of a long-standing nutritional problem. The horse hasn't been getting the nutrients he needs—because he's not being fed properly, because overwork or chronic illness have sapped his strength, or because parasites are helping themselves to his meals. You should be able to feel a horse's ribs (if you can't find them he's too fat) but not see them standing out beneath his skin. Occasionally a poor coat stems from an imbalance of vitamins or a hormone problem.

• Difficulty in breathing can signal various problems, depending on the situation and the type of difficulty. A resting horse who breathes with flared nostrils and obvious effort isn't getting enough oxygen. A serious respiratory infection may be clogging his breathing passages, or he may have a heart or circulatory problem that's slowing the delivery of oxygen to his tissues. Rapid, shallow breathing may indicate overheating (the horse is panting to cool off) or pain from pleurisy or some other cause; if the horse grunts with each breath, he's probably in severe pain. A horse who makes a double effort in exhaling may suffer from heaves.

• Coughing and nasal discharge are usually signs of a respiratory infection, which may be mild or severe. Some clear nasal discharge is normal; be on the lookout for opaque discharge or an increase in quantity. Coughs may also be brought on by dust and pollen.

• A resting pulse over 50 beats a minute may be a sign of

serious trouble: pain, shock, dehydration, or fever. An irregular pulse, on the other hand, may signal heart disease.

• A change in color of the membranes of the gums and nostrils can signal any of several problems. Normally the membranes are a healthy pink. If they're pale, they're not getting enough blood. This is common in colic and in shock, but it may also be a sign of anemia. When the gums and nostrils are really starved for blood, they'll pick up a bluish cast. Fever and dehydration, on the other hand, can turn them deep red. A yellow-brown color may be a sign of kidney or liver disorders or of poisoning.

• Capillary refill time is another indicator of how well the circulatory system is functioning. Press your finger on the horse's gums hard enough to drive the blood out and turn that spot white. If it takes longer than three seconds for the color to return, you can be fairly sure that some problem—low blood pressure, even shock—is interfering with the circulation.

• Foaming at the mouth or nostrils indicates an obstruction in the esophagus. A horse with choke may also duck into his water bucket repeatedly but be unable to drink.

• Difficulty in swallowing can also stem from a sore throat. Sometimes a horse with a sore throat will yawn repeatedly to try and ease the discomfort.

• Swellings around the face point to various problems, not all of them local. An allergic reaction can cause the lips and muzzle to puff up. Hard lumps under the jaw are a sign of strangles—the lymph nodes are infected. Swelling or discharge around the eyes can be signs of an injury or an infection. Another sign of eye inflammation is a nictating membrane drawn partly over the eye.

• Drunken gaits, unusual stumbling, or falling indicate a problem in the central nervous system. When the problem comes on suddenly, it may indicate poisoning; if it follows an accident, it may point to spinal cord injury. Unsteady gaits that develop insidiously can be a sign of wobbler syndrome.

• Muscular tremors in the haunches are a sign of tying up.

The horse has reached the exhaustion point and may have depleted his levels of electrolytes. All-over shivering, on the other hand, can mean that the horse is chilled or is on the verge of a fever.

• Diarrhea can result from a sudden change in feed, but it often indicates an intestinal infection. Hard, dry manure or constipation may stem from fever, too little water, very dry feed, or an underactive thyroid gland. A horse with colic will often pass little or no manure. Blood in the feces is a sign of an ulcer or an acute inflammation in the intestines.

• Changes in urinary output are also trouble signs. Excessive urination points to kidney trouble. When the horse strains to urinate, he may be suffering from an infection or a growth in his urinary tract, or even a bladder stone. When a horse is dehydrated, his urine is concentrated and therefore darker than normal. Very dark urine often follows tying up.

• Unusually restless behavior—the horse paws the floor, gets up and down frequently, rolls, turns to look at or nip his abdomen—signals discomfort, probably from colic. Sometimes a colicky horse will sit on his haunches, like a dog.

• A silent gut—or one that's sounding off like a cannon—also indicates digestive trouble. A horse's normal gut sounds are much like the noise your own stomach makes when it growls.

• A stiff, alert, grinning expression is an early sign of tetanus. Further signs are difficulty swallowing, stiffness throughout the body, nictating membranes drawn over both eyes, and a distinctive straddle-legged stance.

• Bad breath may indicate that the horse has a rotten tooth or infected sinuses. A horse who passes a lot of grain in his manure—or slobbers when he eats so that half of every mouthful falls on the floor—probably needs to have his teeth floated.

• Sweating when work or the weather doesn't warrant it can simply mean that the horse is nervous or upset. If there's no reason for him to be nervous, though, look further: This can also be a sign of colic or poisoning.

• Loss of skin tone is a sign of dehydration. Pinch a small fold of skin and release it; if it doesn't snap back right away, the horse is low in body fluids.

• An unusual stance very often means the horse is in pain. If he stands with his back arched, colic may be the cause. If he stands with his forefeet out in front of his body, he may have laminitis. A horse with laminitis will move reluctantly and with a peculiar, shuffling gait; he's trying to keep weight off his toes. He may or may not run a fever, and you may feel heat in his hoofs.

• A horse that refuses to rise is in serious trouble. Check for serious injury; also consider laminitis.

Chances are that if your horse gets sick, he'll show several symptoms. You won't have to be Sherlock Holmes to add them together and come up with a fairly good picture of what's happening. For example, a bit of nasal discharge and a mildly depressed attitude might point to an upper respiratory infection. Coupled with foul breath, the same symptoms might point to infected sinuses. Or, paired with a fever and difficulty in breathing, they might indicate a much more serious and deeper inflammation, perhaps pneumonia.

A horse with laminitis may stand with his front feet placed in front of his body.

PINPOINTING LAMENESS

One area not covered in the list of symptoms here is lameness, which is in fact one of the troubles your horse is most likely to suffer. Sore legs and feet produce one universal sign: uneven gaits. But there are countless variations of that sign, all indicating different sorts of problems. Being able to distinguish among them will help you determine whether your horse needs a day of rest or immediate veterinary attention.

If you suspect your horse is lame, begin by observing his posture at rest. Normally a horse will stand with his forelegs parallel and weight equally divided between them, and he may rest one or the other hind leg. If he consistently rests one leg, it's probably because he's sore there. How he rests it is another clue. Pointing with one or both forefeet indicates that he's sore in the heel; this is a classic sign of navicular disease. If he holds a leg forward and cocks the knee, suspect fetlock trouble; if the knee is flexed but the foot is behind the vertical, the elbow may be sore. In the same way, a horse with a sore stifle may draw the affected leg under his body to rest it.

Next compare the legs carefully, visually and by touch, checking for cuts, bumps, and signs of inflammation. Work from the sole of the foot right up through the shoulders to the withers—a painful saddle sore can also make the horse travel with uneven gaits. Squishy or puffy areas may point to fresh injuries; unusual heat or stronger pulse, to serious inflammation. (Mild differences in heat are difficult to spot with your hands; some racetrack vets now use thermography, in which the legs are photographed with infrared film, to detect such changes.)

At each point on the leg, press firmly to see if the horse reacts, as he will if he's sore there. If he snatches his leg away, though, compare his reaction to pressure on the same spot in the opposite leg before you decide you've found the trouble— he may just be objecting to your technique. Pick up each leg and flex it to see if joint movement is restricted. Normally a foreleg will flex freely so that the shoe will touch the elbow.

If your close-up exam doesn't turn up any obvious causes for the lameness, watch him in motion. Have someone trot him on a loose lead over level ground. A sound horse holds his head steady as he trots. One with a sore front leg raises his head when that leg meets the ground—he's trying to shift some of his weight back to lighten the load on the leg. A horse with a sore hind leg drops his head when that leg touches down to shift some weight forward. Listen as you watch to determine if one footfall sounds lighter or quicker than the others.

There are other signs, too. When a hind leg is lame, the horse often seems to hike the hip on that side higher than the other as he goes. Front or hind, if a sore muscle or tendon makes it painful for the horse to swing his leg forward, he'll shorten the stride of that leg and bring the foot down early. These so-called swinging-leg lamenesses can sometimes be spotted more easily if the horse is trotted on a gentle slope or soft ground, because this forces him to extend as much as he can and exaggerates any differences between right and left.

On the other hand, if pressure on the leg or foot causes pain—as it will in the case of corns, chip fractures, laminitis, and similar problems—the horse will try to shorten the weight-

A horse with a sore front leg raises his head as that leg meets the ground.

bearing phase of his stride, snatching the foot off the ground as soon as possible so it will be in the air longer. Supporting-leg problems like these often show up more clearly if the horse is trotted on a hard surface. If you trot the horse on a circle, a supporting-leg lameness will often be more pronounced when the sore leg is on the inside, because that leg will have to bear more weight.

Some symptoms point to specific problems. A horse with navicular disease may be lame in both front feet. He'll move with short, stabbing strides as he tries to keep his weight on his toes, and he may stumble frequently. Horses with hock problems travel short and rough behind, poking their toes into the ground as they go. Stifle and hip problems produce a hesitant, dragging stride; often the toe on the affected leg points out. A horse with arthritis often appears to improve after a few minutes of work, as his joints "loosen up," although he really isn't any better. A lameness that comes on suddenly and gets steadily worse, even when the horse is rested, may result from an infection, such as an abscess.

Despite all these telltale signs, though, many lamenesses are nebulous and hard to pin down. If you can't identify the problem, have a vet check the horse. Veterinarians have a variety of diagnostic tools, ranging from hoof testers and flexion tests to nerve blocks and X rays, that can help them pinpoint the problem.

FIRST AID FOR EMERGENCIES

Obviously you won't call a vet out to your barn every time your horse sneezes or bumps his toe. Some situations should be watched for a few days, and some you can handle on your own. Some should be handled by the vet but don't rate the full flashing-light-and-siren treatment. Some qualify as emergencies—they need immediate veterinary attention. Even in situations where you need the vet, though, the care you give the horse can help or hinder his recovery.

Consider it an emergency if your horse shows any symptoms of colic, laminitis, shock, or poisoning. These conditions escalate rapidly, and time is of the essence in treating them. While you're waiting for the vet, try to keep the horse calm and quiet; for colic and laminitis, offer water but no food. It's important to keep a colicky horse from rolling because he may injure himself if he does. Sometimes walking the horse is the only way to accomplish this, although in itself walking does nothing for colic. Some people also advise walking a horse with laminitis to keep circulation moving through the feet, but there are differences of opinion about this. One thing you shouldn't do is give medications unless your vet tells you to. They may obscure the symptoms, so that he can't tell how serious the condition is when he arrives, or they may interfere with drugs he'll want to give.

If a horse appears to be in shock, keep him quiet and do what you can to regulate his temperature until the vet arrives. If the trouble stems from heat exhaustion, get him in the shade; if it's cold, blanket him.

Choke also qualifies as an emergency, and a horse that's bleeding from the nose should be seen promptly by the vet— he could inhale some of the blood and develop pneumonia if the bleeding isn't brought under control. In both cases, keep the horse as quiet as you can while you're waiting for help.

Severe tying up is another emergency condition, because if it's allowed to go on, muscles can be seriously damaged. Here it's important to keep the horse moving, so as much blood as possible circulates through the cramped muscles. Don't try to work the horse (in fact, you probably won't be able to); just walk him slowly. Some trainers administer phenylbutazone or a tranquilizer, but get the advice of your vet first.

Serious injuries—suspected fractures, deep wounds—also need immediate attention. If you must move a horse with a suspected fracture, you should apply an emergency splint. Lengths of PVC pipe, split lengthwise, make good splints, or you can use lengths of boards or broomsticks. Bandage the leg first, with thick padding (you can even use a pillow) under the wrap; then fit the pipe or board over the wrap and secure it with a second bandage.

First aid for wounds has two goals: controlling the bleeding and keeping the wound clean. In most cases bleeding stops on its own in a matter of minutes. If it's copious and just won't stop—because the horse has cut a major vein or artery, for example—you can usually stop it with direct pressure. For a wound on the body, fold a clean cloth and press it on the wound as firmly as you can. For a leg wound, keep the cloth in place with a pressure bandage: Put thick layers of sterile padding over the wound, followed by leg cottons to protect surrounding tissues, and then wrap on a bandage tighter than you normally would. Don't use a tourniquet, which can damage tissues all around the wound by cutting off circulation to them.

If bleeding is under control, clean the wound with plain water—a jet from a hose is fine, or you can use a mild disinfectant solution. The more foreign material in the wound, the greater the chance of infection and the more difficult the healing will be. If there's even an outside chance that a wound will have to be sutured, don't put any kind of medication on it. Suturing will seal in foreign material, and anything trapped inside—including medication—will provoke inflammation and delay healing. When deep wounds can't be sutured, they often fail to heal properly. You end up with an ugly scar or with proud flesh (excessive tissue). In this condition, the healing process runs amok: Instead of the wound filling in and closing over with skin, masses of new tissue form a raw lump. The vet will have to apply caustic medications to cauterize and reduce the lump.

Wounds left open to heal can be dusted with antibiotic powder and bandaged to keep out dirt. Use a sterile no-stick gauze pad over the wound, topped by clean cottons and an elastic bandage that will exert just enough pressure to keep the pad in place (but not so much that circulation is hindered). Avoid greasy medications because dirt may adhere to them. These products are most useful around an open wound, rather than in it, because they prevent the skin from being irritated by drainage from the wound; you can also use petroleum jelly for that purpose.

Not every wound must be seen by a vet, of course. As a general rule, get the vet right away if you can't control bleeding or if the cut is an inch or more long and extends all the way through the skin. And there are two kinds that you shouldn't try to treat on your own, no matter how superficial they seem: punctures, because of the great risk of infection, and eye wounds, because it takes an expert to assess damage to the eye. If your horse gets a puncture, try to keep it open and draining while you're waiting for the vet; a good way to do this is to flush it with antiseptic solution and a syringe.

Conditions that need prompt veterinary attention but don't necessarily qualify as emergencies include mild fever, signs of respiratory illness, and most lameness. Deciding when to call the vet in these cases is largely a question of the severity of the problem. If the horse is coughing and running a fever, you'll want the vet to start treatment as soon as possible. If he has a slight nasal discharge and no other symptoms, you might want to watch him for a day or so. Similarly, if he seems to have a mild, vague lameness, you might decide to just rest him and see if it clears up in a few days—for a stone bruise or a sore muscle, this may well be what the vet advises anyway.

If you detect a pulled muscle in the first day or so, just as the heat and inflammation are starting to build, it may respond well to cold therapy (hosing the leg or bandaging it with some sort of cooling wrap). You can wrap the leg in a regular bandage and wet it (be sure to keep it wet, or it may shrink and cut off circulation as it dries); or bandage the leg and then tape a plastic bag full of ice over the bandage; or use special cold wraps sold in tack shops.

If you're in any doubt as to whether you need professional help, though, your best course is the safe one: Call and get the vet's opinion. Many conditions respond best when treatment is started early, before inflammation gets out of control.

A FIRST AID KIT

Every barn should have a box with basic and emergency medical supplies, and if you trailer or van your horse you should take such a box with you. It should contain the following items, most of which can be found in tack shops, drug stores, or through your vet:

• A mild antiseptic solution or soap, such as betadine or a furacin solution, for cleaning wounds and abrasions
• Sterile gauze or cotton swabs for the same purpose
• A 35-cc syringe for flushing puncture wounds
• Antibiotic dusting powder or spray for wounds that will be left open to heal
• No-stick sterile gauze pads, such as Telfa pads
• Clean leg cottons
• Four-inch elastic bandages, such as Ace bandages, or the self-stick type available from your vet
• Adhesive tape
• Blunt-tipped scissors
• Antibiotic ointment or cream for burns, superficial abrasions, and around open wounds
• Antibiotic eye ointment
• An equine rectal thermometer
• Epsom salts for soaking sore or abscessed feet
• Mild liniment
• A poultice, either premixed or in powder form
• Rubbing alcohol
• Petroleum jelly
• A clean sponge
• Tweezers for removing splinters and the like

Some people also keep split lengths of PVC pipe for making emergency splints, and several drugs, usually an antibiotic such as penicillin, a non-steroidal anti-inflammatory such as phenylbutazone or Banamine, and a mild tranquilizer. Before you use these drugs or any others, though, you should get instructions from your vet on the proper dosage for your horse and the correct method of administration.

2. Managing Problems

If your horse is lame or comes down with any but the mildest illness, getting him back to his usual self will involve special care over a period of weeks or perhaps months. Very likely, you'll work out the specific program of care with your veterinarian—what amount of rest is needed, special feeds or medications, surgical shoeing, and so on. Here are some general principles and procedures to keep in mind.

TROUBLESHOOTING GUIDE

SIGNS	POSSIBLE CAUSES	ACTION
Heat, pain, swelling	inflammation	call vet
Fever	infection	call vet
Low weight, poor coat	improper feeding, parasites	correct diet, deworm
Labored breathing, coughing, etc.	respiratory infection	call vet
Abnormal gum color	anemia; also colic, shock, poisoning, liver or kidney disease	call vet; emergency if colic, shock, or poisoning*
Foaming at mouth or nostrils	choke	call vet*
Difficulty swallowing	sore throat; choke	call vet
Facial swelling	allergy (muzzle); strangles (jaw)	call vet

* Emergency requiring immediate veterinary attention.

SIGNS	POSSIBLE CAUSES	ACTION
Incoordination	wobbler syndrome; injury; poisoning	call vet; emergency if injury or poison*
Tremors in haunches; unwilling to move	tying up	walk horse; call vet*
Shivering	chilled; fever	stable and blanket horse; check temperature
Diarrhea	feed change; infection	return to normal feed; call vet for infection
Dry manure or none	dry feed; too little water; colic	give water; change feed; call vet* for colic
Change in urine; straining	kidney trouble; dehydration	give water; call vet
Restlessness; discomfort; rolling; nipping at flanks	colic	call vet* keep horse quiet; prevent rolling
Abnormal gut sounds	colic	same as above*
Stiffness; grinning expression; sawhorse stance	tetanus	call vet* keep horse quiet
Foul breath	rotten tooth; sinus infection	call vet
Sweating without reason	fever; colic; poisoning	call vet*
Loss of skin tone	dehydration	offer water and electrolytes; call vet*
Odd stance; shuffling gait; unwilling to move	laminitis	call vet*
Heat and increased pulse in feet	laminitis	call vet*
Refuses to rise	laminitis or severe injury	call vet*
Uneven gaits: Sudden, severe Mild, insidious	injury; infection; various lamenesses	call vet* rest horse; call vet to evaluate

* Emergency requiring immediate veterinary attention.

REST

Rest is the first step in curing any injury or illness. In fact, you needn't wait for your vet's advice to put this part of the program into effect. Anytime you suspect your horse is ill or lame, play it safe and rest him at least until you get a clearer picture of what's ailing him. If it turns out that nothing was wrong, he won't have been harmed by having a day off; if the problem is serious, you at least won't have made it worse.

Turning a horse out in a pasture or a paddock isn't a good way to rest him, because most horses (unless they're very ill) don't have the sense to limit their exercise. For an infectious disease or for the initial, inflammatory stage of a lameness, the vet will probably prescribe stall rest. And when a horse is confined to a stall for a long period of time—as he may be with a fracture, a badly injured tendon, or an infectious illness —you'll want to make him as comfortable as you can.

Choose the largest box you can find, so he'll have room to stretch his limbs and will be in less danger of getting cast if he lies down and tries to roll. Make sure he has ample bedding. Since he's in the stall all day and night, the bedding will probably get dirty faster than it ordinarily would, so pick up the stall at least twice a day. If he has a respiratory infection, use bedding that's as close to dust-free as possible. Diced newsprint (which is sold in bales especially for this purpose) works well. It's also important that the stall be well ventilated, so the horse won't be breathing stale barn air all day. But watch out for drafts that could chill him, and in cold weather make sure he's blanketed.

Isolation usually isn't necessary, even with most infectious diseases. By the time your horse shows symptoms, every horse in the barn has probably already been exposed to his germs. You shouldn't bring new horses into the barn while he's ill, however (and you should thoroughly disinfect the stable when he's recovered). Still, while he's feeling low he'll probably appreciate being in a somewhat out-of-the-way corner, where he won't be continually disturbed and excited by comings and goings. That may change as time goes on and he begins to feel better; then boredom may lead him to start chewing the wood in his stall, weaving, or indulging in some other stable vice. Move him to a spot where he can see other horses and get a good view of what's going on in the barn.

If he's well enough, the vet may tell you to hand-walk him for a certain amount of time each day. A horse that hasn't been exercised in a while can be a veritable volcano of pent-up energy. Take some precautions to protect yourself and to keep him from injuring himself in his enthusiasm. Walking him in his bridle, or with the chain end of the lead line looped over his nose, will give you an extra bit of control. Pick a route that offers minimum excitement, not along the fence of a paddock where other horses are bucking and playing.

When a long period of rest and recuperation is called for, the vet may advise turnout. This depends on the nature of the injury, the temperament of the horse, and the climate. Turnout can be a boon to a horse with a chronic respiratory problem, such as heaves, because it keeps him away from aggravating stable dust and fumes. Some mild and chronic lamenesses also improve when the horse can spend his days moving about naturally, particularly if he's a placid type who won't injure himself galloping around. Turning him out with a quiet and congenial pasturemate can help keep him calm (some horses become frantic when they're in a field alone).

With rare exceptions, though, the idea that under-saddle work will help a mild lameness is a mistaken one. A horse with an arthritic problem will appear to get better as he works. In fact, this is one sign veterinarians look for in diagnosing such conditions. Just as humans who have arthritis are stiffest in the morning when they get out of bed, the horse is stiffest when he comes out of his stall. But forcing the joints to work, while it may make the horse seem better, can produce wear and tear and actually aggravate the disease. Sometimes this is the goal —the vet may order work for a hock problem, for example, to aggravate the arthritis and help the joint fuse faster. But usually the inflammation provoked by work is to be avoided, and the horse is better off resting.

One of the most common mistakes people make is putting the horse back to work too soon. He'll look and act normal long before he's completely healthy, and since he can't talk he won't be able to tell you that his throat is still a bit scratchy or that he still feels a twinge in his right ankle every so often. Loading on work too soon can put you right back where you started. Just when and how you bring the horse back to work is something to plan carefully with your vet. A respiratory infection may require a month of rest; badly torn ligaments or tendons, a year or more. In any event, bear in mind that a long period of rest allows all the horse's muscles and tendons to grow weak. You'll have to build him back to his former level of fitness slowly, watching extra carefully for signs of lameness as you go.

FEEDING

A horse that's resting doesn't need the level of energy he needs when he's in work, and his rations should be adjusted accordingly. In fact, they must be, or you'll be courting laminitis or colic. Switch him onto good quality grass hay, which will provide everything he needs for maintenance while he's resting, and eliminate his grain, which has too high a concentration of energy. As with all changes in feed, though, make the switch gradually, increasing the hay ration and cutting back on grain over a period of several days.

The horse can have all the hay he wants, and nibbling on it may help him pass time and avert boredom while he's confined. But follow his regular feeding schedule, giving the hay at the usual time. If other horses are getting grain at feeding time, he may be upset; try putting some alfalfa pellets, which have a low energy level, in his bucket to quiet him. Pellets are also useful in you're not satisfied with the quality of your hay.

If the horse is too ill to take an interest in hay or pellets, you have a problem—he must keep eating, both to keep his strength up for recovery and to keep his intestines working properly. He may find pellets more appealing if you mix them with finely chopped apples and carrots. Many horses can be tempted to eat a bran mash or a mixture of dampened bran and sweet feed, both of which have a higher fiber content than grain alone. Beet pulp is another high-fiber, low-energy feed that many horses find appetizing; because it's dust-free, it's often fed as a hay substitute to horses with heaves. Be sure to soak the pulp in water for a full twenty-four hours and then squeeze out excess water before you feed it, or the pulp can expand inside the horse's intestines and bring on a case of colic.

While you'll cut the quantity of carbohydrates the horse eats while he's resting, you'll want to be sure that he gets the full amount of vitamins, minerals, and protein that he needs for tissue repair. The requirements for these components don't vary as much with work as does the requirement for energy. Again, a pelleted ration can be useful, especially if the only available hay isn't up to par. The ration will also give you a vehicle for medications or supplements that your vet may prescribe.

MEDICATIONS

If your horse needs medications, your vet will probably instruct you in how and when to administer them. This will save him frequent trips to your barn (and will save you the fees for recurrent barn calls). The two classes of drugs most commonly prescribed for a wide range of equine problems are antibiotics and anti-inflammatories of various types. It's worthwhile understanding how these drugs work and how they should be administered.

Antibiotics were developed from natural substances that kill bacteria and fungi. Some are specific; they knock out only a few bugs but do so efficiently. Others, such as penicillin, are broad-spectrum, affecting many germs. Very often a vet will prescribe a broad-spectrum drug at the outset of an infection and then, if need be, switch to another antibiotic after identifying (through a laboratory analysis) what agent is at work.

One of the main reasons for making antibiotic therapy as specific as possible is that many bacteria are helpful to the horse, especially those that aid his digestion; there's no sense in killing them all. Another reason is that bacteria can develop resistance to a drug. A few bacteria aren't affected by it and live to reproduce; their offspring are also able to resist the drug, and so the infection worsens. Bacteria also have the ability to swap genetic material with unrelated bacteria. That means that harmless intestinal bacteria can grow resistant to penicillin, for example, and then pass on this resistance to harmful bacteria that enter the gut.

Whatever antibiotic is prescribed, it's extremely important to stick to the dosage schedule ordered by the vet. Some antibiotics work by killing bacteria outright; others stop them from reproducing. Especially with the second, bacteriostatic type, it's essential to keep enough drug circulating at all times. Unhindered, some bacteria can double in number in less than an hour. Suppose, for example, your vet has ordered antibiotics every eight hours, at 6:00 A.M., 2:00 P.M., and 10 P.M. If you decided to lump your horse's midday dose together with his morning one for the sake of convenience, the extra drug might not harm him. But his system might have metabolized all the drug by midafternoon, leaving the bacteria half the afternoon and most of the evening in which to multiply.

To minimize their effect on the horse's digestion, antibiotics are often given by injection rather than orally. Giving a horse an intramuscular injection isn't difficult. Your vet can show you how to find the "safe" zones and give you the necessary materials.

Nonsteroidal anti-inflammatories are among the drugs most commonly given to horses. Most of these drugs work on the same principle: They inhibit the production of prostaglandins, body chemicals that are involved in the inflammatory process. Phenylbutazone (informally called "bute") is often prescribed because it's cheap and usually works. Flunixin meglumine (Banamine) and naproxen are also used. These drugs are most useful in cooling down the initial stages of an injury or lameness, because when inflammation gets out of hand it can complicate healing. They aren't painkillers per se, but because pain is part of the inflammatory response they help reduce it. They're of less use as time goes on, for several reasons. First, a certain amount of inflammation helps (and in fact is necessary for) healing. Next, reducing inflammation artificially makes it difficult to judge how healing is progressing—the injury is masked. Still, these drugs can be useful in managing chronic conditions like arthritis, provided they're given judiciously.

Bute in particular (because of its low cost) is overused in a lot of barns—handed out like candy at the first signs of soreness, or given routinely before competitions. But none of the anti-inflammatories is free of side effects (studies have shown that high doses of bute over time produce ulcers and possibly liver and kidney damage), so they should never be given without veterinary supervision. One way to detect side effects early is to test the horse's level of blood protein at the outset of treatment and then repeat the test periodically. A drop in the value may indicate that an ulcer has formed. You should also watch the horse carefully for a loss of appetite or a listless attitude, both of which can be early signs of trouble.

A typical starting dose of bute is two grams twice a day for a 1,000-pound horse, an amount that's quickly cut back to the lowest dose that allows the horse to be comfortable. Bute is usually given in tablets that are crushed in feed (or in an oral paste) because injections can be dangerous—if the shot goes into a vein by mistake, the horse can collapse. Banamine can be more safely given by injection.

Corticosteroids are prescribed less often because they pose

more risks than the nonsteroidal anti-inflammatories. These drugs mimic natural body chemicals, produced by the adrenal cortex, that halt inflammation. Because they also stifle the horse's immune response, they aren't given when infection is present or right after vaccination. Giving steroids systemically (in feed or by injection) for longer than three days creates the danger that, with the immune system suppressed, new infections will take hold. And since the adrenal cortex won't produce any natural corticosteroids while the drug is present, it may atrophy in long-term therapy. When the drug is withdrawn, the horse becomes listless and drops weight; in an extreme case he might even die.

Local steroid injections are sometimes used to reduce inflammation in muscle and tendon injuries, on the theory that these injuries will then heal with less scarring. One or two such injections may not hurt, but repeated treatments can interfere seriously with healing. Steroids also have a dramatic effect when injected into sore joints, but, again, over time they can actually promote the deterioration of the joint. For this reason some promising new drugs, such as hyaluronic acid, have largely taken their place in treating arthritis and similar conditions. These or any other drugs injected into a joint should, of course, be handled by a vet because of the great risk of introducing infection into the joint capsule.

An important point to remember in using any anti-inflammatory is that the medication treats symptoms, not the underlying cause of the problem. The primary purpose of using the drug is to control inflammation and make the horse as comfortable as possible while rest or some other therapy works its healing effects. And as long as the horse is on anti-inflammatories, his symptoms won't give you an accurate picture of his health. You won't be able to tell whether he's trotting sound because he's better or because the drug has reduced inflammation. You'll have to take him off medication entirely and wait a day or two for the drug to clear from his system before you can decide.

WRAPS, LINIMENTS, AND OTHER LEG TREATMENTS

If your horse has wrenched supporting tendons and ligaments in a leg, your vet may tell you to keep him in support bandages, at least during the early stages of healing. A support bandage is applied like a stable bandage, using an elasticized wrap, and takes over some of the functions of the injured tissues. Even when the injury affects only one leg, the vet may suggest you wrap the opposite leg as well. The reason is that when one leg is sore, the horse will put more weight than usual on the opposite leg, and he may injure that one, too.

Whirlpooling, or hydrotherapy, has become a popular treatment, especially for chronic leg problems. There are whirlpool boots, for soaking one leg, and whirlpool tubs, which can take two legs at a time. The bubbling, swirling water acts like a gentle massage, and after some initial hesitation most horses learn to enjoy it.

Along with wraps, many people apply liniments and leg preparations of one kind or another. How much good they do is a subject of debate; some vets say that many of these concoctions do more to soothe the owner's state of mind than to heal the horse's leg. Most liniments and leg paints work on the same principle: They create heat, which theoretically increases circulation to the injured area and thus speeds healing. However, a preparation that's put on the skin will have most of its effect at skin level; the increase in circulation to injured tissues underneath will be minimal at best.

In most leg preparations, the heat is created by counter-irritants—ingredients in the liniment that irritate the skin—so you'll obviously keep these products out of open wounds. They also shouldn't be used when heat is present in the leg—the injury is already inflamed, and you'd do better to cool things down with water or an alcohol brace. The time to use liniments is after the initial inflammation has died down.

Mild liniments usually produce their heating effect with various plant oils, such as camphor. Leg paints and blisters, which are much stronger, may contain caustic chemicals that actually burn the skin. These products have been widely used to treat serious injuries, such as bowed tendons and arthritic lumps. But their real benefit may be that they force the owner to rest the horse while he's in treatment. Some newer techniques, such as therapeutic ultrasound and diathermy (which uses radio waves) have produced better results with soft-tissue injuries.

Dimethyl sulfoxide (DMSO) is a solvent that has become popular as a liniment in recent years; it's less irritating to the skin than some and has the ability to carry medications (such as anti-inflammatories) through the skin to the deeper tissues. If you use it, get it through your vet rather than buying the industrial grade, which may contain impurities.

Poultices and sweats are used to reduce swelling, either through cold (for a fresh injury) or heat (for an old one). They work, although you're treating symptoms, not the cause of the swelling. The basic ingredient in most poultices is clay; it's mixed with water, applied to the affected area, and covered with plastic wrap and a bandage to keep it moist for a period of hours. Some poultices contain mild counterirritants; sweats generally contain stronger ones, usually in a glycerine base, and are put on in more or less the same way as poultices.

Some treatments extend the counterirritant theory to deeper tissues. In pinfiring, which is sometimes done for chronic tendon and ankle soreness, a hot needle penetrates the skin to create inflammation below. Internal blistering agents are sometimes injected directly into arthritic joints. In tendon splitting, small surgical incisions are made in a bowed tendon. The idea behind all of these techniques is to draw blood to the area by increasing inflammation and thereby promote better healing.

Again, there's debate, and there's logic on both sides. It's true that tendons, joints, and similar areas are often less well served by circulation than muscles are. Often, healing in these tissues seems to grind to a halt before the job is done. It's logical that stirring things up a bit might keep the process going longer and perhaps make it more complete (although none of these techniques can start healing up again once it has halted completely). The other side of the coin is that the techniques basically create additional injury, which can leave the horse with more scar tissue (and thus a weaker tendon or whatever) than he might otherwise have had.

MANAGING CHRONIC PROBLEMS

Just like people, horses aren't young forever, and as they get older they may start to develop aches and pains and other conditions that limit them. An accidental injury can also leave the horse with some degree of permanent disability, great or small. While good care, proper conditioning, and reasonable workloads will forestall many such problems, nothing can guarantee that your horse will be free of them for life. That doesn't mean, though, that he'll be washed up if he gets a touch of arthritis; you can work around many mild disabilities with adjustments in your care and work schedules.

One treatment that shouldn't be overlooked is surgical shoeing. A horse that's resting can in many cases have his shoes pulled and will be the better for it; after that, careful shoeing can speed recovery. Farriers have moved away from the sort of "corrective" shoeing that was designed to make every equine foot conform to set angles and flight paths, recognizing that most horses do better if their feet are left as nature designed them. But a great deal can be done with shoes to make a horse that's recovering from a lameness, or one that's chronically lame, more comfortable.

Pads can protect sensitive soles that are prone to bruising. Some of the newer pads also use the same sort of shock-absorbing material that's used in jogging shoes; they may reduce concussion throughout the foot. Shoeing full in the heels or grooving the hoof wall at the quarters, so they will expand more easily, can help horses with sidebone and similar problems. Degree pads can be used to raise sore heels and take some pressure off them. Bar shoes of various designs (in which the open end of the shoe is closed by a metal bar) also relieve pressure and are often used on horses with navicular disease or laminitis. Simply rolling the toes of the shoes can help a horse with sore heels a great deal, because it will allow his feet to break over faster and thus get weight off the heels sooner.

One of the most direct methods of dealing with chronic unsoundness is to adjust the horse's workload. As obvious as this seems, many people don't think of it. The fact that a day in the hunt field leaves a horse sore and aching, though, doesn't mean that he can't instead hack through the countryside for an hour or two in perfect comfort. In setting a work schedule for a chronically sore horse, let his symptoms be your guide— don't do anything that, based on previous experience, might leave him lame. If you overdo it while you're attempting to find the right level of work and provoke a flare-up of his condition, an anti-inflammatory can help make him comfortable until the episode passes.

Many people use these drugs to keep a chronically lame horse in full work, administering them before or after schooling sessions and competitions (depending on the regulations of the organization running the competition). This course is a matter of personal choice. It wouldn't be mine because it seems unkind to keep a horse in work on drugs if he could be sound doing less without them, and there is also the risk that, with symptoms masked, the horse will injure himself more seriously. However, a lot of mitigating circumstances persuade people to keep a horse going on painkillers or anti-inflammatories of one sort or another: The horse is exceptionally talented, the owners have invested a fortune in him, and so on. The "right" course probably depends on the individual situation.

Keeping a horse with a chronic problem going requires extra time and effort—walking, massaging and wrapping legs, giving medications, soaking beet pulp for the horse with heaves. It also requires extra money—for special shoes, feed, or bedding and for vet calls. Not every owner will find it worthwhile or even possible to provide the special care required in every case. What's important to remember is that it's not necessary to write off a horse when a chronic health problem develops. If the extra care can be given, it often pays off handsomely in years of extended performance.

CHAPTER VII

Living Proof

One of the most captivating stories from the 1984 Los Angeles Summer Olympics was that of Keen, the 17.2-hand chestnut thoroughbred gelding owned and ridden by dressage competitor Hilda Gurney of California. Neither Gurney nor Keen were new to international competition. They had led the U.S. Olympic dressage team to a bronze medal in Montreal in 1976, and they had earned both team and individual golds in the 1979 Pan-American Games in Puerto Rico. But two factors made their 1984 appearance remarkable: Keen was eighteen years old, and he had staged one of the most surprising equine comebacks on record.

Gurney had bought Keen as a three-year-old and had painstakingly trained him to the point where, in the mid- and late 1970s, he was considered one of the top dressage horses in the world. Then, not long after his triumph in the 1979 Pan-American Games, disaster struck. In a freak riding accident, the horse pulled ligaments in both front legs and damaged nerves in his spinal cord. The ligaments healed, but the nerve damage seemed permanent. Barely able to hobble around,

Keen was turned out to pasture at Gurney's farm. His career was thought to be over.

Nearly four years passed with no sign of improvement in the gelding. Gurney turned her attention to training other mounts. Then, one day in 1983, she turned a broodmare into Keen's pasture. To her surprise, the gelding began to chase the mare—with no sign of lameness in his gait. Veterinarians confirmed what she had seen: the damaged nerves had healed. Keen went back to work in August of that year, and Gurney slowly and carefully built him up to the point where, in June 1984, he was winning Grand Prix competitions and earned himself and his owner a spot on the Olympic team. Of the U.S. entries at Los Angeles, they scored the highest.

Keen's story has an element of luck; no one expected the horse to return to work. But for the most part it illustrates the results of patience and good care. And while his recovery from the spinal injury may be unusual, he's far from being the only older horse to make an impressive showing in competition. While Keen was trying out for the dressage team, for example, two other teenagers were strong contenders for the three-day-event team: Kim Walnes's Gray Goose, fourteen, and Torrance Fleischmann's Laser, fifteen. California quarter horse trainer Mariel Hannay qualified another fifteen-year-old, Valley Host, for the quarter horse World Championship in western riding, and the gray gelding (owned by Carole Hooper Clark) made a strong showing there. And the American Horse Show Association's junior jumper of the year in 1984 was the eighteen-year-old Doc O'Day, owned and ridden by Scott Novick—who at sixteen was younger than his horse.

Outside the rarified levels of top competition, stories of older horses who keep right on going are legion. A typical tale involves a Massachusetts woman who decided to keep her daughter's Appaloosa mare when the daughter went off to college. The mare was in her late teens when she began to learn the difficult movements of dressage. Similarly, a California rider bought a thoroughbred off a school string; he was nine years old and virtually crippled from rope burns. He recovered, and eleven years later was not only sound but sporting dapples and a glow of good health. And these horses are mere babies compared to some other old campaigners: Another California thoroughbred was showing in his twenties and didn't retire from work until the distinguished age of thirty-six. A Pennsylvania hunter followed the hounds regularly until, at age twenty-three, he bowed a tendon. But while the injury took him out of the hunt field, it didn't end his career. At thirty-five, he was still taking his now-retired owner for hacks through the countryside.

There are many other such stories. They're still exceptions—for every horse that's still working late in life, dozens wash up by the time they reach their teens. It's commonplace for a horse to star on the show circuit or in the hunt field for a season or two and then never be heard from again. Accidents and diseases take their toll, but in many cases these horses could have lasted longer. They didn't because they were over-matched with work and poorly trained and conditioned, or because their basic daily care was neglected. They may have started their careers well—perhaps even won major competitions—but eventually, they paid the bills for their owners' mistakes.

The theme of this book has been that horse owners wouldn't make such mistakes if they understood their animals' needs. The formula for a sound and healthy horse is relatively simple:

• First, know the horse's limits and set goals that fit within them—don't plan a career in dressage if you know the horse has weak hocks.

• Second, condition the horse to the level of fitness he needs for his sport and keep him there.

• Third, never stint when it comes to the level of daily care and nutrition—a small saving in time and money can buy you a lot of heartache down the road.

• And fourth, be an alarmist—watch constantly for signs of trouble and take action immediately when you spot them.

Those four basic steps, coupled with a sprinkling of good luck, can make your horse the lifetime investment and companion you'd like him to be.

Author's Note

Sports medicine for humans is a relatively new field; for equine athletes, it's newer still. Readers who want to know more about the topics covered in this book will find that much material on horse care is sadly out of date. However, some good sources are available.

The full National Research Council recommendations for equine nutrition are available from the Printing and Publishing Office, National Academy of Sciences, 2101 Constitution Avenue, N.W., Washington, D.C. 20418. Ask for *Nutrient Requirements of Horses*. Dr. Harold Hintz of Cornell University, who helped prepare the report, is also the author of an excellent and thoroughly up-to-date book on the subject, *Horse Nutrition: A Practical Guide* (New York: Arco, 1983).

For detailed how-to instructions on daily grooming, Susan Harris's *Grooming to Win* (New York: Scribners, 1977) is hard to beat. The book also gives thorough descriptions of show-ring turnout for hunter, Western, saddlebred, and other events, as well as tips on caring for show tack.

Where lameness and illness are concerned, as well as the nitty-gritty of physiological functions, veterinary texts tend to be the most thorough and up-to-date. Unfortunately, most are also close to impenetrable without a good grounding in medical terminology. Among the more solid and readable is *Lameness in Horses* by O. R. Adams (Philadelphia: Lea & Febiger), first published in 1962 and revised several times since then. If you're the sort of person who keeps a copy of *Physician's Desk Reference* in the house to consult when you get a prescription, you might take an interest in Thomas Tobin's *Drugs and the Performance Horse* (Springfield: Thomas, 1981). Tobin, one of the leading researchers in the field, presents a comprehensive account of how most medications affect horses.

As of this writing several major veterinary schools have ongoing research projects in the areas of exercise stress and conditioning, as well as in horse health care generally. Results of such projects are often reported first in the magazines and journals directed at horsemen; they are good sources for information in this field, which is changing rapidly.

It was in the course of writing such articles for one of these magazines, *Practical Horseman*, that the idea for this book occurred to me. Collecting material for it spanned several years and brought me in contact with veterinarians and researchers around the country; I'm indebted to each of them. Among those who were especially patient in answering what to them must often have seemed simplistic questions were Dr. G. Frederick Fregin, director of the Marion DuPont Scott Equine Medical Center in Leesburg, Virginia; Dr. Michael Collier and Dr. Herbert Schryver of Cornell University; Dr. William Moyer of the University of Pennsylvania's New Bolton Center; and Dr. Gerald Auman of Delaware Equine Center in Cochranville, Pennsylvania.

The horse world is fortunate to have people like these working as practitioners in the field and as researchers behind the scenes. Equine veterinary researchers in particular are a singularly dedicated crew, doing remarkable work often under severe funding restraints. If in the future horses' lives are easier and longer, it will be largely because of their efforts.

Index